PRENTICE HALL

WORLD GEOGRAPHY

BUILDING A GLOBAL PERSPECTIVE

Guide to the Essentials
Teacher's Manual

Includes

- **Answers to All Review and Test Questions in** *Guide to the Essentials* **in English and Spanish**

- **Strategies for Reaching Students of Varying Abilities**

- **Letter Home in English and Spanish**

Section-by-Section Reading Support

Prentice
Hall

Contents

To the Teacher 3

Teaching Students of Varying Abilities 5

Letter home in English 8

Letter home in Spanish 9

Answer Key for Guide to the Essentials 10

Answer Key for Spanish Edition 17

ISBN 0-13-062507-8

3 4 5 6 7 8 9 10 06 05 04 03

TO THE TEACHER

The *Guide to the Essentials* is designed to provide students with the most essential content in their world geography course in an easy-to-follow format.

Each page in the *Guide to the Essentials* contains

- a summary of key content;

- a graphic organizer, such as a web, flow chart, map, or time line;

- highlighted vocabulary words and social studies terms that are defined in context and appear in the Glossary at the back of the book;

- comprehension questions.

There is a test at the end of each chapter to assess student understanding.

The Spanish Edition contains

- translations of the *Guide to Essentials* text summaries and related questions;

- translations of the chapter tests;

- a Spanish/English glossary.

- translation of the index

You may use the *Guide to the Essentials* as a

- preview to help focus reading in the content area

- review of content to prepare students for assessment

- quick summary when circumstances require it

In addition, Guided Reading Audiotapes that include pre-reading questions as well as the summaries from the *Guide to the Essentials* are available in English and Spanish.

TEACHING STUDENTS OF VARYING ABILITIES

Kari Bryski

Petaluma Junior High School, Petaluma, California

Teaching social studies in innovative and creative ways to students with diverse linguistic and cultural backgrounds is a challenge. It requires a mind open to new possibilities, strategies, and points of view. In a heterogeneous classroom, students bring varying levels of experience and knowledge to the classroom. Students may have relevant information from another class but may not be able to make the connection with what they are reading. As a social studies teacher, you must help your students to see these links and to develop a wider perspective of the world around them.

STRATEGIES AND TECHNIQUES

The following teaching tools have proven effective in supplementing English texts in diverse classrooms. Though only the basics, they are a good place to begin. Whether you use the English or Spanish version of the *Guide to the Essentials,* there are techniques you can use to enhance your students' study of world geography. Many of the following methods are used commonly by educators all across the country. Keep in mind that *any* strategies that activate and connect the learner's prior knowledge to new information in a meaningful way are valuable.

- Use brainstorming in cooperative groups (where first language can be used to communicate) or pairs to discover prior knowledge.

- Use graphic organizers (e.g., "What do you know? What do you want to know? What did you learn?" charts or Venn diagrams) to show the connection of content to prior understanding and to build background knowledge that is meaningful.

- Have students skim a reading assignment and make an outline from the headings and subheadings. Suggest that they leave space for notes.

Activate and develop students' prior knowledge

- Decide what the essential concepts are in the lesson, and focus on teaching one or two.

- Find out what insights students have about the concepts (e.g., *How does the environment affect jobs in your community?*).

> *"Any strategies that activate and connect the learner's prior knowledge to new information . . . are valuable."*

Develop key vocabulary

- Define key vocabulary and terms before the lesson begins.

- Help students learn vocabulary by using context clues.

- Define key terms by example, description, or compare and contrast.

- Use familiar synonyms, appositives, or clues that illustrate the origin of the term.

- Help students recognize terms that are similar in other languages.

- Help students use the key terms to make a tree map or writing web showing the relationships among people, terms, and events.

Use heterogeneous student teams or cooperative learning groups

- Every group should have a mix of gender, learning styles, and abilities.

- Integrate English language learners into the groups with English speakers.

Present lessons with strong contextual support that is easy to understand and makes new information meaningful.

- Focus on thematic content relevant to student experience and/or interest.

- Use a variety of materials that teach to varied learning styles.

- Make use of graphic organizers, art, and other visuals in conjunction with the lesson.

- Personalize the instruction by asking students referential questions, eliciting their opinions, and encouraging them to share related personal experiences.

- Ask students working in pairs to explain the key elements of the reading to one another.

Summarize and highlight key concepts in a visual record that students also record.

- Help students organize the information from the lesson in an outline, chart, concept web, or notes.

- Let students test their understanding by writing a summary based on their outline, chart, concept web, or notes.

- Have students make a story board for a movie or television show based on the important people and concepts from the reading.

> *"The task is to make the social studies content comprehensible to everyone."*

THE MULTILINGUAL CLASSROOM

You may be one of an increasing number of teachers who face the challenge of working in a multilingual environment. Some students may lack English comprehension or speaking skills but be skilled in another language. In some cases, students may lack skills in both English and their native language.

Students from every corner of the world can have ethnic and linguistic perspectives that differ as much from each other's as they do from that of mainstream American students. In a multicultural setting, prior knowledge about any topic can vary widely. In addition, students may know relevant information in their first language, but not recognize a connection with what they are reading in English. The task is to make the social studies content comprehensible to everyone.

Educators have recommended a number of strategies and techniques for addressing the multilingual classroom. The good news is that many of these strategies are familiar and already part of many teachers' arsenals. The strategies described above, for example, will address the needs of all students— English speakers and English language learners alike. There are, in addition, a number of other ways to reach out to and challenge your multilingual students.

Create a learning environment where students feel safe to share culture, language, and personal ideas as they explore new concepts and languages. Encourage active language use.

- Openly identify, acknowledge, and accept diversity in the classroom by honoring individual rights to be respected, regardless of language or culture differences.

- Help English language learners understand what you say by using gestures, dramatic expression, and role-playing to communicate meaning.

- Use assorted manipulatives and props.

- Begin the study of a subject by having students look at the visuals to gain a general understanding of the content.

- Encourage students to use the glossary or a bilingual dictionary to acquire the social studies words related to the topic.

Ask questions and develop performance-based assessments that require higher-order thinking skills

- Maintain clear speech, good enunciation, and simpler syntax when speaking.

- Avoid the use of idioms.

- Have students work in teams or cooperative learning groups to create products and performances that synthesize and evaluate information.

> *"Success in a multilingual classroom is a matter of finding the right tools to bridge the gap between what students know and what they must learn."*

In the multilingual, heterogeneous classroom, all students are capable of learning the same academic content. Research shows that success in a multilingual classroom is a matter of finding the right tools to bridge the gap between what students know and what they must learn. These tools include effective teaching strategies and the educator's creative use of them. The result will be student academic achievement that motivates everyone to further participate in the learning process. It is a progressive cycle, and it is your challenge to teach it creatively.

Dear Family Member,

This year, your son or daughter will be using a Prentice Hall Social Studies program. That program pays careful attention to the unique characteristics and development needs of adolescents. As a parent, you undoubtedly realize that adolescents need support in *all* areas of development.

All students will face challenges over the coming school year. To help them prepare to meet the challenges of a rigorous World Geography curriculum, I will be assigning work in the *Guide to the Essentials of World Geography* throughout the semester. These worksheets will help students preview the textbook, review essential content, prepare for exams, and successfully complete the required coursework.

Home involvement is a vital part of the education process. I encourage you to take an active role by showing interest in your child's progress. By staying involved, you show your child that you value education and the effort your child is giving to his or her schoolwork.

Sincerely,

Teacher

Querido miembro de la familia:

Este año, su hijo o hija va a usar un programa de Estudios Sociales de Prentice Hall. Este programa presta una atención cuidadosa a las características y necesidades únicas del desarrollo de los adolescentes. Como padre o madre, usted sin duda se da cuenta de que los adolescentes necesitan apoyo en todas las áreas de su desarrollo.

Todos los estudiantes van a enfrentarse a muchos retos durante el próximo año escolar. Para ayudarles a prepararse a superar las exigencias de un riguroso programa de Geografía Universal, voy a ir asignanado trabajo de la *Guía Básica de la Geografía Universal* durante este semestre. Estas hojas de trabajo ayudarán a los estudiantes a examinar el libro de texto, revisar el contenido esencial, preparar exámenes y completar con éxito la tarea escolar necesaria.

La participación de los miembros del hogar es una parte vital del proceso educativo. Le animo a participar activamente mostrando interés en el progreso de su hijo o hija. Al participar, le muestra a su hijo o hija que usted valora la educación y el esfuerzo que él o ella pone en el trabajo escolar.

Sinceramente,

El profesor/La profesora

ANSWERS TO
GUIDE TO THE ESSENTIALS
REVIEW AND TEST QUESTIONS

Chapter 1 **Review Questions**

p. 5
1. location, place, human-environment interaction, movement, regions
2. Europe, Africa

p. 6
1. 70 percent
2. inner core, outer core, mantle, and crust

p. 7
1. Weathering is the process of breaking down rock into smaller pieces; erosion is the movement of weathered materials from one place to another.
2. mechanical weather, chemical weathering

Chapter 1 Test p. 8

1. A	6. C
2. B	7. D
3. D	8. A
4. D	9. B
5. A	10. D

Chapter 2 **Review Questions**

p. 9
1. Any three of the following: latitude, wind patterns, ocean currents, precipitation, elevation, nearby bodies of water and landforms
2. from northeast to southeast and from southeast to northwest

p. 10
1. forest, grassland, desert, and tundra
2. low bushes

Chapter 2 Test p. 11

1. B	6. A
2. C	7. C
3. A	8. A
4. D	9. B
5. C	10. C

Chapter 3 **Review Questions**

p. 12
1. in cities
2. about two billion

p. 13
1. A monarch's power is hereditary and comes from being born into a ruling family. A democratic leader's power comes from being elected by citizens.
2. command economy

Chapter 3 Test p. 14

1. A	6. A
2. D	7. C
3. C	8. B
4. C	9. D
5. A	10. B

Chapter 4 **Review Questions**

p. 15
1. Possible answer: Recycling makes it possible to reuse some minerals that would have been thrown out.
2. Possible answer: Water power will never be used up because it is renewable. Oil will be used up someday.

p. 16
1. Possible answer: In subsistence farming farmers raise only enough for themselves and their village. In commercial farming, farmers raise crops and animals to sell and can feed more people.
2. tertiary activity

Chapter 4 Test p. 17

1. C	6. B
2. A	7. C
3. D	8. D
4. B	9. B
5. C	10. A

Chapter 5 **Review Questions**

p. 18
1. Possible answers: Rocky Mountains, continental divide, interior plains
2. Arctic Ocean, Pacific Ocean, Atlantic Ocean

Chapter 5 Test p. 19

1. D	**6.** A
2. B	**7.** D
3. C	**8.** B
4. D	**9.** D
5. C	**10.** B

Chapter 6 Review Questions

p. 20

1. Possible answers: rich farmland, forests, minerals, water
2. rich natural resources, good transportation and communications systems, free-enterprise system, hardworking people

p. 21

1. Many goods were shipped across the Atlantic to and from Europe.
2. village

Chapter 6 Test p. 22

1. A	**6.** D
2. C	**7.** A
3. C	**8.** B
4. B	**9.** D
5. D	**10.** D

Chapter 7 Review Questions

p. 23

1. They provided water power and routes for transportation.
2. Maine, New Hampshire, Massachusetts, Rhode Island, Connecticut, New York, and New Jersey

p. 24

1. Possible answer includes any two: mild climate, rich soil, oil, space industry
2. Texas, Louisiana, Mississippi, Alabama, and Florida

p. 25

1. The Midwest has many very productive farms.
2. Minnesota, Wisconsin, Illinois, Indiana, Michigan, Ohio

p. 26

1. Los Angeles uses aqueducts to bring in water.
2. Pacific Ocean

Chapter 7 Test p. 27

1. D	**6.** A
2. C	**7.** D
3. A	**8.** B
4. B	**9.** A
5. B	**10.** D

Chapter 8 Review Questions

p. 28

1. The Great Lakes–St. Lawrence region. (Other acceptable answers: Ontario and Quebec or the St. Lawrence Lowlands)
2. Alberta, Saskatchewan, and Manitoba

p. 29

1. They want Quebec to be an independent country.
2. Britain

p. 30

1. Possible answer: The challenge is to develop the resources without harming the environment.
2. The United States has a higher GDP.

Chapter 8 Test p. 31

1. B	**6.** A
2. C	**7.** D
3. D	**8.** C
4. A	**9.** A
5. C	**10.** D

Chapter 9 Review Questions

p. 32

1. market economy, command economy, and traditional economy
2. Pacific Ocean, Caribbean Sea

Chapter 9 Test p. 33

1. B	**6.** B
2. A	**7.** C
3. C	**8.** D
4. C	**9.** D
5. D	**10.** A

Chapter 10 Review Questions

p. 34

1. the central plateau
2. Baja California

p. 35

1. oil and tourism
2. ancient Indian, colonial Spanish, and modern Mexican

Chapter 10 Test p. 36

1. A	**6.** B
2. B	**7.** D
3. B	**8.** A
4. C	**9.** B
5. D	**10.** C

Chapter 11 Review Questions

p. 37
1. farming
2. Guatemala, Honduras, Nicaragua, Costa Rica, and Panama

p. 38
1. windward islands
2. Caribbean Sea, Atlantic Ocean, Gulf of Mexico

Chapter 11 Test p. 39

1. B
2. C
3. B
4. A
5. C
6. A
7. B
8. B
9. B
10. D

Chapter 12 Review Questions

p. 40
1. the Southeast
2. Manaus

p. 41
1. It has given away land and mining permits and built roads.
2. It increased from 60% in 1974 to 78% in 1994.

Chapter 12 Test p. 42

1. C
2. B
3. D
4. D
5. C
6. A
7. A
8. B
9. C
10. C

Chapter 13 Review Questions

p. 43
1. Venezuela
2. tierra templada

p. 44
1. Chile
2. Bolivia

p. 45
1. Argentina
2. Paraguay, Argentina, and Bolivia

Chapter 13 Test p. 46

1. D
2. B
3. A
4. B
5. C
6. C
7. A
8. D
9. C
10. B

Chapter 14 Review Questions

p. 47
1. Economic growth in Western Europe has encouraged people to migrate to the region.
2. Germany

Chapter 14 Test p. 48

1. A
2. B
3. B
4. A
5. D
6. C
7. B
8. A
9. D
10. B

Chapter 15 Review Questions

p. 49
1. the Midlands
2. England, Scotland, Wales, and Northern Ireland

p. 50
1. the Central Lowlands
2. Scotland

p. 51
1. Catholic and Protestant
2. 1949

p. 52
1. an economy in which the government operates some businesses and private companies operate others
2. Norway, Sweden, and Finland

Chapter 15 Test p. 53

1. B
2. C
3. B
4. A
5. A
6. C
7. B
8. A
9. C
10. D

Chapter 16 Review Questions

p. 54
1. the Paris Basin
2. Belgium, Luxembourg, Germany, Switzerland, Monaco

p. 55
1. The Ruhr Valley is rich in coal and produces most of Germany's iron and steel.
2. the Alps

p. 56
1. for agriculture
2. the Netherlands

p. 57
1. World War I
2. a little over 100,000

Chapter 16 Test p. 58

1. A
2. D
3. B
4. B
5. C
6. B
7. B
8. D
9. A
10. C

Chapter 17 Review Questions

p. 59
1. Iberian Peninsula
2. Atlantic Ocean

p. 60
1. to find jobs in factories
2. the Alps

p. 61
1. Possible answer: It is on the Mediterranean Sea and it shares its history and geography with other Mediterranean countries.
2. Italy; Portugal

Chapter 17 Test p. 62

1. A	**6.** A
2. D	**7.** B
3. A	**8.** C
4. C	**9.** B
5. C	**10.** D

Chapter 18 Review Questions

p. 63
1. Flat broad plains have made movement across the region easy.
2. Russia

Chapter 18 Test p. 64

1. C	**6.** A
2. B	**7.** C
3. D	**8.** B
4. A	**9.** C
5. B	**10.** C

Chapter 19 Review Questions

p. 65
1. Their religion and their attachment to the land helped the Poles keep their national identity.
2. Gdańsk location on the Baltic Sea makes it an important port.

p. 66
1. They all had Communist governments.
2. the Danube River

p. 67
1. to break up into small unfriendly countries
2. five countries

p. 68
1. They have diversified and privatized their industries and encouraged foreign investment and trade.
2. Ukraine; Moldova

Chapter 19 Test p. 69

1. C	**6.** A
2. C	**7.** C
3. C	**8.** D
4. D	**9.** B
5. A	**10.** C

Chapter 20 Review Questions

p. 70
1. fertile soil in the grasslands of Russia
2. Moscow

p. 71
1. *glasnost* and perestroika
2. Mongols overrun Kievan state.

p. 72
1. more than 80 percent
2. The United States; its per capita GDP is more than 11 times that of Russia.

Chapter 20 Test p. 73

1. A	**6.** B
2. B	**7.** D
3. D	**8.** A
4. A	**9.** C
5. A	**10.** D

Chapter 21 Review Questions

p. 74
1. Judaism, Christianity, and Islam
2. Iran, Turkmenistan, Kazakhstan, Azerbaijan

Chapter 21 Test p. 75

1. C	**6.** B
2. B	**7.** D
3. A	**8.** A
4. B	**9.** D
5. C	**10.** B

Chapter 22 Review Questions

p. 76
1. the systematic killing or intentional destruction of a people
2. Georgia

p. 77
1. Islam
2. Kazakhstan

Chapter 22 Test p. 78

1. D	**6.** C
2. C	**7.** A
3. A	**8.** D
4. A	**9.** A
5. D	**10.** D

Chapter 23 Review Questions

p. 79
1. Jews and Arabs
2. Iraq, Palestine, Trans-Jordan

p. 80
1. Possible answer: The desert has been irrigated and swamps have been drained.
2. Egypt, Jordan, Syria, and Lebanon

p. 81
1. Possible answer: Jordan lost its fertile farmland to Israel after the 1967 war.
2. 1948, 1956, 1967, 1973, 1982

p. 82
1. They know that the oil will run out one day.
2. Saudi Arabia

p. 83
1. Possible answer: Atatürk overthrew Turkey's sultan and made Turkey a republic; he began to modernize the nation and separated the Islamic religion and the government.
2. Iran

Chapter 23 Test p. 84

1. A	**6.** B
2. C	**7.** A
3. C	**8.** D
4. D	**9.** B
5. C	**10.** A

Chapter 24 Review Questions

p. 85
1. a huge desert that separates North Africa from the rest of Africa
2. East and Southern Africa

Chapter 24 Test p. 86

1. B	**6.** C
2. B	**7.** A
3. A	**8.** B
4. D	**9.** D
5. B	**10.** C

Chapter 25 Review Questions

p. 87
1. They live near the Nile because the land there is fertile.
2. machinery and equipment

p. 88
1. Libya and Algeria
2. Algeria and Libya

Chapter 25 Test p. 89

1. B	**6.** C
2. D	**7.** A
3. B	**8.** D
4. A	**9.** A
5. A	**10.** B

Chapter 26 Review Questions

p. 90
1. the process of turning land to desert
2. the Songhai Empire

p. 91
1. a sudden political takeover of a government
2. Atlantic Ocean

p. 92
1. Possible answer: After the price of oil fell, Nigeria needed money.
2. 110,532,242

p. 93
1. Possible answer: It is a source of food and water and a means of transportation.
2. Central African Republic

Chapter 26 Test p. 94

1. A	**6.** C
2. D	**7.** C
3. B	**8.** D
4. A	**9.** A
5. C	**10.** C

Chapter 27 Review Questions

p. 95
1. Possible answer: *Harambee* means "pulling together." It meant people in Kenya worked together to build a strong economy.
2. Sudan

p. 96
1. Eritrea
2. Red Sea, Gulf of Aden

p. 97
1. Possible answer: Apartheid was the system of laws in South Africa that segregated black South Africans.
2. Any two: Sanctions placed against South Africa; Prime Minister de Klerk promises reforms; Mandela released from jail; apartheid laws ended; new constitution guarantees equal rights; Mandela becomes president.

p. 98
1. Possible answer: Zambia depended on the sale of copper to buy food. When the price of copper dropped, Zambia did not have money to buy enough food.
2. Namibia, Botswana, Zimbabwe, Mozambique, Swaziland, and Lesotho

Chapter 27 Test p. 99

1. C	**6.** D
2. B	**7.** A
3. D	**8.** D
4. A	**9.** D
5. C	**10.** B

Chapter 28 Review Questions

p. 100
1. The Himalayas
2. The west coast gets most of the summer monsoon rains.

Chapter 28 Test p. 101

1. C	**6.** A
2. A	**7.** B
3. B	**8.** C
4. C	**9.** D
5. B	**10.** A

Chapter 29 Review Questions

p. 102
1. Nonviolent resistance is opposing an enemy without using violence.
2. 80 percent

p. 103
1. Possible answer: Many Indians believe they have more opportunity in cities.
2. farmers and merchants

p. 104
1. Possible answer: The Indus River provides irrigation and hydroelectric power.
2. Sri Lanka

Chapter 29 Test p. 105

1. A	**6.** A
2. D	**7.** B
3. C	**8.** C
4. C	**9.** B
5. B	**10.** D

Chapter 30 Review Questions

p. 106
1. farming that requires much labor to produce food
2. Possible answer: Australia and Antarctica are located south of East Asia.

Chapter 30 Test p. 107

1. B	**6.** A
2. B	**7.** D
3. C	**8.** A
4. D	**9.** C
5. C	**10.** B

Chapter 31 Review Questions

p. 108
1. Possible answer: China's people and economy suffered.
2. Possible answers: during World War II; from 1937 to 1945.

p. 109
1. the Northeast
2. Northeast, Southeast, Northwest, Southwest

p. 110
1. Possible answer: It encouraged one-child families, rewarding people who had just one child and punishing those who had more.
2. around 1980

p. 111
1. Taiwan
2. Taiwan

Chapter 31 Test p. 112

1. A	**6.** B
2. C	**7.** B
3. B	**8.** A
4. C	**9.** A
5. D	**10.** C

Chapter 32 Review Questions

p. 113
1. Possible answer: a common heritage, language, and religion
2. Kyushu, Shikoku, Honshu, and Hokkaido

p. 114
1. Japan imports raw materials and exports finished goods.
2. People are highly educated, companies encourage loyalty and team spirit, the government takes an active role in business, and Japan is located at the center of trade routes.

p. 115
1. Possible answer: The Soviet Union was in charge of the northern part of Korea, and the United States was in charge of the southern part. The Soviets set up a Communist government in the north, and the people in the south held elections.
2. South Korea

Chapter 32 Test p. 116

1. D	**6.** A
2. B	**7.** C
3. A	**8.** C
4. D	**9.** A
5. C	**10.** D

Chapter 33 Review Questions

p. 117
1. Buddhism, Hinduism, and Islam
2. Indian, Muslim, Chinese, and European

p. 118
1. Possible answer: Vietnam began looking for foreign investments, and its economy boomed.
2. All their cultures were influenced by India, most of their people are Buddhists, and all three were once known as French Indochina.

Chapter 33 Test p. 119

1. C
2. B
3. D
4. A
5. D

6. B
7. C
8. C
9. B
10. A

Chapter 34 Review Questions

p. 120
1. Aborigines, probably from Southeast Asia.
2. Perth, Darwin, Brisbane, Sydney, Melbourne, Adelaide, and Hobart

p. 121
1. The Maori were the first people to settle in New Zealand.
2. Fiji

p. 122
1. Possible answer: No country had permanent settlers there, and the nations of the world wanted to share Antarctica.
2. Mining, military activities, nuclear explosions, disposals of radioactive waste

Chapter 34 Test p. 123

1. D
2. C
3. A
4. D
5. C

6. B
7. A
8. D
9. D
10. B

RESPUESTAS PARA LA
GUÍA DE LOS ELEMENTOS ESENCIALES
PREGUNTAS DE REPASO Y DE LAS PRUEBAS

Capítulo 1 Preguntas de repaso

pág. 5

ubicación, lugares, interacción humana con el medio ambiente, movimiento, regiones

pág. 6

el 70 por ciento

pág. 7

Intemperización es el proceso de ruptura de las rocas con lo cual se forman pedazos más pequeños; la erosión es el movimiento de los materiales intemperizados de un lugar a otro.

Prueba del capítulo 1 pág. 8

1. A	**6.** C
2. B	**7.** D
3. D	**8.** A
4. D	**9.** B
5. A	**10.** D

Capítulo 2 Preguntas de repaso

pág. 9

Cualesquiera tres de los siguientes: la latitud, los patrones de los vientos, las corrientes oceánicas, la precipitación, la altura, las masas de agua y otros terrenos que hay en las cercanías.

pág. 10

el bosque, la pradera, el desierto y la tundra

Prueba del capítulo 2 pág. 11

1. B	**6.** A
2. C	**7.** C
3. A	**8.** A
4. D	**9.** B
5. C	**10.** C

Capítulo 3 Preguntas de repaso

pág. 12

en las ciudades

pág. 13

El poder del monarca es hereditario y le pertenece a quienes nacen de la familia gobernante. El poder de un dirigente democrático proviene de su elección por los ciudadanos.

Prueba del capítulo 3 pág. 14

1. A	**6.** A
2. D	**7.** C
3. C	**8.** B
4. C	**9.** D
5. A	**10.** B

Capítulo 4 Preguntas de repaso

pág. 15

Una respuesta posible: Con el reciclaje se pueden volver a utilizar algunos minerales que se hubieran tirado.

pág. 16

Una respuesta posible: En la agricultura de subsistencia, los agricultores solamente cultivan lo suficiente para sus propias familias y aldeas. En la agricultura comercial, los agricultores siembran cosechas y crían animales para vender y pueden alimentar a más personas.

Prueba del capítulo 4 pág. 17

1. C	**6.** B
2. A	**7.** C
3. D	**8.** D
4. B	**9.** B
5. C	**10.** A

Capítulo 5 Preguntas de repaso

pág. 18

Posibles respuestas: las Montañas Rocosas, la línea divisoria continental, las planicies interiores

Prueba del capítulo 5 pág. 19

1. D	**6.** A
2. B	**7.** D
3. C	**8.** B
4. D	**9.** D
5. C	**10.** B

Capítulo 6 Preguntas de repaso

pág. 20

Las posibles respuestas: ricos suelos, bosques, minerales, agua

pág. 21

Muchos productos se transportaban por el Atlántico hasta y desde Europa.

Prueba del capítulo 6 pág. 22

1. A	**6.** D
2. C	**7.** A
3. C	**8.** B
4. B	**9.** D
5. D	**10.** D

Capítulo 7 Preguntas de repaso

pág. 23

Proporcionaron energía hidráulica y rutas de transporte.

pág. 24

Una posible respuesta incluye dos de los siguientes elementos: el clima suave, los ricos suelos, el petróleo, la industria espacial

pág. 25

El Medio Oeste tiene muchas granjas muy productivas.

pág. 26

Los Ángeles trae agua por medio de acueductos.

Prueba del capítulo 7 pág. 27

1. D	**6.** A
2. C	**7.** D
3. A	**8.** B
4. B	**9.** A
5. B	**10.** D

Capítulo 8 Preguntas de repaso

pág. 28

en la zona de los Grandes Lagos y el Río San Lorenzo (Otras respuestas aceptables: Ontario y Quebec o las Tierras Bajas del San Lorenzo)

pág. 29

Quieren que Quebec sea un país independiente.

pág. 30

Una respuesta posible: El reto es aprovechar los recursos sin perjudicar el medio ambiente.

Prueba del capítulo 8 pág. 31

1. B	**6.** A
2. C	**7.** D
3. D	**8.** C
4. A	**9.** A
5. C	**10.** D

Capítulo 9 Preguntas de repaso

pág. 32

las economías de mercado, centralizada y tradicional

Prueba del capítulo 9 pág. 33

1. B	**6.** B
2. A	**7.** C
3. C	**8.** D
4. C	**9.** D
5. D	**10.** A

Capítulo 10 Preguntas de repaso

pág. 34

en la meseta central

pág. 35

el petróleo y el turismo

Prueba del capítulo 10 pág. 36

1. A	**6.** B
2. B	**7.** D
3. B	**8.** A
4. C	**9.** B
5. D	**10.** C

Capítulo 11 Preguntas de repaso

pág. 37

la agricultura

pág. 38

las islas de barlovento

Prueba del capítulo 11 pág. 39

1. B	**6.** A
2. C	**7.** B
3. B	**8.** B
4. A	**9.** B
5. C	**10.** D

Capítulo 12 Preguntas de repaso

pág. 40

el sureste

pág. 41

Regaló terrenos, confirió permisos de explotación minera y edificó carreteras.

Prueba del capítulo 12 pág. 42

1. C	**6.** A
2. B	**7.** A
3. D	**8.** B
4. D	**9.** C
5. C	**10.** C

Capítulo 13 Preguntas de repaso

pág. 43

Venezuela

pág. 44

Chile

pág. 45

Argentina

Prueba del capítulo 13 pág. 46

1. D	**6.** C
2. B	**7.** A
3. A	**8.** D
4. B	**9.** C
5. C	**10.** B

Capítulo 14 Preguntas de repaso

pág. 47

El crecimiento económico en Europa Occidental ha alentado a la gente a migrar a la región en busca de empleo.

Prueba del capítulo 14 pág. 48

1. A	**6.** C
2. B	**7.** B
3. B	**8.** A
4. A	**9.** D
5. D	**10.** B

Capítulo 15 Preguntas de repaso

pág. 49

las tierras medias

pág. 50

en las tierras bajas centrales

pág. 51

la católica y la protestante

pág. 52

economía en la cual el gobierno maneja algunos negocios y otros son manejados por compañías privadas

Prueba del capítulo 15 pág. 53

1. B	**6.** C
2. C	**7.** B
3. B	**8.** A
4. A	**9.** C
5. A	**10.** D

Capítulo 16 Preguntas de repaso

pág. 54

la cuenca de París

pág. 55

La Valle del Ruhr es rico en carbón y produce la mayor parte del hierro y acero de Alemania.

pág. 56

las usan para la agricultura

pág. 57

La Primera Guerra Mundial

Prueba del capítulo 16 pág. 58

1. A	**6.** B
2. D	**7.** B
3. B	**8.** D
4. B	**9.** A
5. C	**10.** C

Capítulo 17 Preguntas de repaso

pág. 59

en la península ibérica

pág. 60

para encontrar empleos en fábricas

pág. 61

Una respuesta posible: Está al borde del Mar Mediterráneo y compare su historia y geografía con otros países mediterráneos.

Prueba del capítulo 17 pág. 62

1. A	**6.** A
2. D	**7.** B
3. A	**8.** C
4. C	**9.** B
5. C	**10.** D

Capítulo 18 Preguntas de repaso

pág. 63

Las llanuras anchas y planas han facilitado movimiento a través de la región.

Prueba del capítulo 18 pág. 64

1. C	**6.** A
2. B	**7.** C
3. D	**8.** B
4. A	**9.** C
5. B	**10.** C

Capítulo 19 Preguntas de repaso

pág. 65

Su religión y su amor por la tierra hay ayudado a los polacos a mantener su identidad nacional.

pág. 66

Todos tenían gobiernos comunistas.

pág. 67

dividirse en pequeños países hostiles

pág. 68

Han diversificado y privatizado sus industrias y han fomentado las inversiones y el comercio del extranjero.

Prueba del capítulo 19 pág. 69

1. C	**6.** A
2. C	**7.** C
3. C	**8.** D
4. D	**9.** B
5. A	**10.** C

Capítulo 20 Preguntas de repaso

pág. 70
suelo fértil de las llanuras rusas

pág. 71
glasnost y perestroika

pág. 72
más del 80 por ciento

Prueba del capítulo 20 pág. 73

1. A	**6.** B
2. B	**7.** D
3. D	**8.** A
4. A	**9.** C
5. A	**10.** D

Capítulo 21 Preguntas de repaso

pág. 74
el judaísmo, el cristianismo y el islam

Prueba del capítulo 21 pág. 75

1. C	**6.** B
2. B	**7.** D
3. A	**8.** A
4. B	**9.** D
5. C	**10.** B

Capítulo 22 Preguntas de repaso

pág. 76
la matanza sistemática o destrucción intencional de un pueblo

pág. 77
Islam

Prueba del capítulo 22 pág. 78

1. D	**6.** C
2. C	**7.** A
3. A	**8.** D
4. A	**9.** A
5. D	**10.** D

Capítulo 23 Preguntas de repaso

pág. 79
los judíos y los árabes

pág. 80
Una respuesta posible: Han irrigado el desierto y se han drenado los pantanos.

pág. 81
Una respuesta posible: Después de la guerra de 1967, Jordania perdió ante Israel sus fértiles tierras agrícolas.

pág. 82
Porque saben que algún día se les agotará el petróleo.

pág. 83
Una respuesta posible: Atatürk derrocó al sultán de Turquía y convirtió a Turquía en república; comenzó a modernizar a la nación y separó la religión islámica del gobierno.

Prueba del capítulo 23 pág. 84

1. A	**6.** B
2. C	**7.** A
3. C	**8.** D
4. D	**9.** B
5. C	**10.** A

Capítulo 24 Preguntas de repaso

pág. 85
un enorme desierto que separa el norte de África del resto de África

Prueba del capítulo 24 pág. 86

1. B	**6.** C
2. D	**7.** A
3. A	**8.** D
4. A	**9.** D
5. B	**10.** B

Capítulo 25 Preguntas de repaso

pág. 87
Viven cerca del Río Nilo porque la tierra es fértil allí.

pág. 88
en Libia y Argelia

Prueba del capítulo 25 pág. 89

1. B	**6.** C
2. D	**7.** A
3. B	**8.** D
4. A	**9.** A
5. A	**10.** B

Capítulo 26 Preguntas de repaso

pág. 90
el proceso por el cual la tierra se convierte en desierto

pág. 91
una toma repentina del poder político del gobierno

pág. 92
Una respuesta posible: Cuando el precio del petróleo cayó, a Nigeria le hizo falta dinero.

pág. 93
Una respuesta posible: Es una fuente de alimentos, agua y transporte.

Prueba del capítulo 26 pág. 94

1. A	**6.** C
2. D	**7.** C
3. B	**8.** D
4. A	**9.** A
5. C	**10.** C

Capítulo 27 Preguntas de repaso

pág. 95

Una respuesta posible: *Harambee* quiere decir "el trabajo conjunto". Significa que la gente en Kenia trabajaba en forma colectiva con el fin de formar una economía fuerte.

pág. 96

Eritrea

pág. 97

Una respuesta posible: Apartheid fue el sistema de leyes en Sudáfrica mediante el cual se segregaron los negros de los blancos.

pág. 98

Una respuesta posible: Zambia contaba con el dinero proveniente de la exportación de cobre para comprar alimentos. Cuando cayó el precio del cobre, a Zambia le hizo falta dinero para comprar alimentos suficientes.

Prueba del capítulo 27 pág. 99

1. C	**6.** D
2. B	**7.** A
3. D	**8.** D
4. A	**9.** D
5. C	**10.** B

Capítulo 28 Preguntas de repaso

pág. 100

La cordillera del Himalaya

Prueba del capítulo 28 pág. 101

1. C	**6.** A
2. A	**7.** B
3. B	**8.** C
4. C	**9.** D
5. B	**10.** A

Capítulo 29 Preguntas de repaso

pág. 102

La resistencia no violenta quiere decir oponerse a un enemigo sin emplear la violencia.

pág. 103

Una respuesta posible: Muchos de los habitantes de la India creen que en las ciudades tienen más oportunidades.

pág. 104

Una respuesta posible: El Río Indo es fuente de potencia hidroeléctrica y agua para riego.

Prueba del capítulo 29 pág. 105

1. A	**6.** A
2. D	**7.** B
3. C	**8.** C
4. C	**9.** B
5. B	**10.** D

Capítulo 30 Preguntas de repaso

pág. 106

agricultura que requiere de mucha mano de obra para producir comida

Prueba del capítulo 30 pág. 107

1. B	**6.** A
2. B	**7.** D
3. C	**8.** A
4. D	**9.** C
5. C	**10.** B

Capítulo 31 Preguntas de repaso

pág. 108

Una respuesta posible: Tanto el pueblo como la economía de China sufrieron.

pág. 109

el noreste

pág. 110

Una respuesta posible: Animó a las familias a tener un solo hijo, y premió a las personas que tenían un solo hijo y castigó a las personas que tenían más.

pág. 111

Taiwan

Prueba del capítulo 31 pág. 112

1. A	**6.** B
2. C	**7.** B
3. B	**8.** A
4. C	**9.** A
5. D	**10.** C

Capítulo 32 Preguntas de repaso

pág. 113

Una respuesta posible: un mismo legado, idioma y religión

pág. 114

Japón importa materias primas y exporta bienes acabados.

pág. 115

Una respuesta posible: La Unión Soviética se encargó de la parte norteña de Corea y Estados Unidos se encargó de la parte sureña. Los Soviéticos instalaron un gobierno comunista en el norte y en el sur, la gente celebró elecciones.

Prueba del capítulo 32 pág. 116

1. D	**6.** A
2. B	**7.** C
3. A	**8.** C
4. D	**9.** A
5. C	**10.** D

Capítulo 33 Preguntas de repaso

pág. 117

el budismo, el hinduísmo y el islam

pág. 118

Una respuesta posible: Vietnam empezó a buscar inversiones del extranjero y su economía floreció.

Prueba del capítulo 33 pág. 119

1. C	**6.** B
2. B	**7.** C
3. D	**8.** C
4. A	**9.** B
5. D	**10.** A

Capítulo 34 Preguntas de repaso

pág. 120

Los aborígenes, probablemente del sureste de Asia.

pág. 121

Los maoríes fueron los primeros en poblar a Nueva Zelanda.

pág. 122

Una respuesta posible: Ningún país tenía habitantes permanentes ahí, y las naciones del mundo querían compartir a la Antártida.

Prueba del capítulo 34 pág. 123

1. D	**6.** B
2. C	**7.** A
3. A	**8.** D
4. D	**9.** D
5. C	**10.** B

ISBN 0-13-062507-8

00000

9 780130 625076

See us on the Internet | PHSchool.com

PRENTICE HALL

WORLD GEOGRAPHY

BUILDING A GLOBAL PERSPECTIVE

Guide to the Essentials

PEARSON
Prentice
Hall

Upper Saddle River, New Jersey
Glenview, Illinois
Needham, Massachusetts

TO THE TEACHER

The *Guide to the Essentials* for *World Geography: Building a Global Perspective* is designed to provide students with the most essential content in their world geography course in an easy-to-follow format. The text summaries and graphic organizers will help students organize key information. Vocabulary terms are highlighted and defined in the text narrative, as well as in the glossary. A chapter test at the end of each chapter checks students' understanding of the basic content.

You may wish to use the *Guide to the Essentials* as a preview or review of textbook chapters covered in the course, or as a summary of textbook chapters that cannot be studied in detail because of time considerations.

CONTENT CONSULTANTS

Thomas J. Baerwald
Program Director for Geography
National Science Foundation
Arlington, Virginia

Celeste Fraser
Geography Education Specialist
Chicago, Illinois

READING CONSULTANT

Bonnie Armbruster
Professor of Education
University of Illinois at Urbana-Champaign
Urbana, Illinois

ISBN 0-13-062504-3
4 5 6 7 8 9 10   07 06 05 04 03

Contents

UNIT 1 — Physical and Human Geography

Chapter 1	Exploring Geography	5
Chapter 2	Climates and Ecosystems	9
Chapter 3	Population and Culture	12
Chapter 4	Resources and Land Use	15

UNIT 2 — The United States and Canada

Chapter 5	Regional Atlas: Introduction to the United States and Canada	18
Chapter 6	A Profile of the United States	20
Chapter 7	Regions of the United States	23
Chapter 8	Canada	28

UNIT 3 — Latin America

Chapter 9	Regional Atlas: Introduction to Latin America	32
Chapter 10	Mexico	34
Chapter 11	Central America and the Caribbean	37
Chapter 12	Brazil	40
Chapter 13	Countries of South America	43

UNIT 4 — Western Europe

Chapter 14	Regional Atlas: Introduction to Western Europe	47
Chapter 15	The British Isles and Nordic Nations	49
Chapter 16	Central Western Europe	54
Chapter 17	Mediterranean Europe	59

UNIT 5 — Central Europe and Northern Eurasia

Chapter 18	Regional Atlas: Introduction to Central Europe and Northern Eurasia	63
Chapter 19	Central and Eastern Europe	65
Chapter 20	Russia	70

UNIT 6 — Central and Southwest Asia

Chapter 21	Regional Atlas: Introduction to Central and Southwest Asia	74
Chapter 22	The Caucasus and Central Asia	76
Chapter 23	The Countries of Southwest Asia	79

UNIT 7 Africa

Chapter 24 Regional Atlas: Introduction
to Africa   85
Chatper 25 North Africa   87
Chapter 26 West and Central Africa   90
Chapter 27 East and Southern Africa   95

UNIT 8 South Asia

Chapter 28 Regional Atlas: Introduction to
South Asia   100
Chapter 29 The Countries of South Asia   102

UNIT 9 East Asia and the Pacific World

Chapter 30 Regional Atlas: Introduction
to East Asia and the Pacific
World   106
Chapter 31 China   108
Chapter 32 Japan and the Koreas   113
Chapter 33 Southeast Asia   117
Chapter 34 The Pacific World
and Antarctica   120

Glossary   124

Index   130

Exploring Geography

SECTION 1 — THE STUDY OF GEOGRAPHY

■ TEXT SUMMARY

Geography is the study of where people, places, and things are located and how they relate to each other. Geographers use a variety of geographic tools, including maps, charts, and computer and satellite technologies. Geographers use concepts, or ideas, to organize the way they think about geography.

Many geographers use five main themes to study geography. The theme of location describes where a place is found. A location may be an **absolute location**, or its position on the globe. **Relative location** describes where a place is in relation to another place. An example of relative location is, "Mexico is south of the United States."

The theme of place describes how areas are alike or different. Places can be described by their physical features or in terms of their human characteristics, or how people live there.

The third geographic theme deals with regions. A region is a group of places with at least one thing in common. Geographers divide the world into many different regions based on various criteria.

The theme of movement describes the ways people, goods, and ideas move from one place to another. Geography has an important effect on movement.

The final geographic theme examines how people use and change their environment. People expand areas by building homes, roads, and factories, which have positive and negative effects on the surroundings.

> **THE BIG IDEA**
>
> Geographers use five themes, or ideas, to organize their study of the earth and its people.

■ GRAPHIC SUMMARY: *The World: Continents and Oceans*

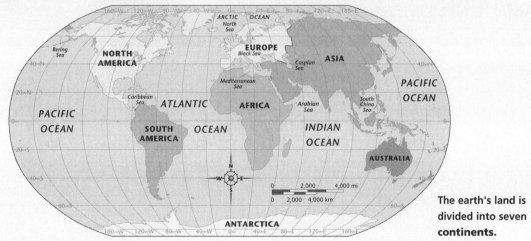

The earth's land is divided into seven **continents.**

■ REVIEW QUESTIONS

1. Name the five themes of geography.

2. **Map Skills** Which two continents are bordered on the west by the Atlantic Ocean?

CHANGES WITHIN THE EARTH

◼ TEXT SUMMARY

Forces of nature, like volcanoes, are constantly changing the earth. Geology is the study of the earth's history and physical structure.

The center of the earth is called the **core**. It is made of very hot metal. The inner core is probably solid, while the outer core is liquid. The **mantle** is a thick layer of rock around the core. The **crust** is the earth's rocky outside layer. It is very thin, like the icing on a cake.

More than 70 percent of the earth's surface is covered by water, mostly oceans and seas. The seven **continents** are the largest areas of land.

Forces inside the earth shape the earth's landforms. Volcanoes, for example, are mountains that form when molten, or melted, rock inside the earth breaks through the crust. On the surface, the molten rock flows as lava.

Breaks in the earth's crust cause faults. Sudden movement along a fault can cause an earthquake.

Most geologists believe that the earth's landmasses have broken apart, rejoined, and moved apart again. According to the theory of **plate tectonics**, the earth's crust and upper mantle are broken into moving plates. These plates can pull apart, crash into each other, or slide past each other. Oceans and continents ride on top of the plates.

> ### THE **BIG** IDEA
>
> **The earth is always changing. Changes that take place inside the earth cause changes in the shape of the land.**

◼ GRAPHIC SUMMARY: *The Earth's Layers*

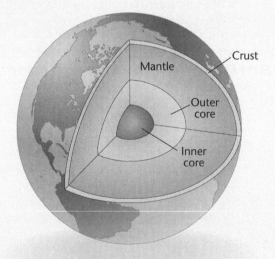

Crust
Mantle
Outer core
Inner core

Scientists believe that the earth has several layers.

◼ REVIEW QUESTIONS

1. How much of the earth's surface is water?

2. Diagram Skills What are the four layers of the earth?

 **SECTION 3** CHANGES ON THE EARTH'S SURFACE

◼ TEXT SUMMARY

The surface of the earth is constantly changing. The forces that change the earth's surface are usually grouped into two categories: weathering and erosion.

Weathering is the process of breaking down rock into smaller pieces. **Mechanical weathering** breaks down or weakens rocks physically. Ice is the chief cause of mechanical weathering. Ice widens cracks and splits rocks.

Chemical weathering changes the chemical makeup of rocks. Water and carbon dioxide are the main causes of chemical weathering. They combine to form an acid that can dissolve rocks.

Erosion is the movement of weathered materials, such as soil, sand, and gravel, from one place to another. Moving water is the major cause of erosion. The water carries pieces of rock that act like sandpaper, grinding away the surface of rocks. Then the moving water carries away the bits of rocks and soil and deposits them elsewhere.

Wind is another cause of erosion. Winds lift away soil that has little to hold it. Then the winds deposit the soil elsewhere. Sand in the wind can carve or smooth the surfaces of rocks.

Glaciers, or slow-moving sheets of ice, are another cause of erosion. They wear away land and move rocks and soil to other places. Glaciers have carved out lakes and valleys.

> **THE BIG IDEA**
>
> **Two forces that change the surface of the earth are weathering and erosion.**

◼ GRAPHIC SUMMARY: *Weathering and Erosion*

	WEATHERING		EROSION		
	MECHANICAL	CHEMICAL	MOVING WATER	WIND	GLACIERS
WHAT IT DOES	• Physically breaks down large pieces of rock	• Changes a rock's chemical makeup	• Cuts into rock and wears it away • Carries pieces of rock to other places	• Carries soil away and deposits it elsewhere	• Carry dirt, rocks, and boulders • Wear away land
EXAMPLES	• Frozen water expands and enlarges cracks • Seeds fall into cracks and grow into trees that split the rocks	• Acid created by water and carbon dioxide can dissolve rocks • Acid rain eats away rock surfaces	• Carves canyons and valleys • Creates flood plains and deltas	• Dust bowls are formed by loss of soil • Rich farmland is created by new deposits of soil	• Carved out the Great Lakes

Weathering and erosion are the main causes of change in the earth's surface.

◼ REVIEW QUESTIONS

1. What is the difference between weathering and erosion?

2. Chart Skills What are two kinds of weathering?

CHAPTER 1 *Test*

▣ IDENTIFYING MAIN IDEAS

Write the letter of the correct answer in the blank provided. (10 points each)

____ **1.** Which of the following is the study of places, how they affect people, and how people change them?
   A. geography
   B. movement
   C. region
   D. climate

____ **2.** The theme of place describes
   A. exact location.
   B. how areas are alike or different.
   C. relative location.
   D. how goods are moved.

____ **3.** A group of places with at least one thing in common form a
   A. location.
   B. relative location.
   C. government.
   D. region.

____ **4.** Geology is the study of
   A. the earth's plants and animals.
   B. how roads and factories are built.
   C. how ships and airplanes carry people.
   D. the earth's history and structure.

____ **5.** What is the name of the center of the earth?
   A. core
   B. fault
   C. earthquake
   D. lava

____ **6.** The theory that the earth's crust is broken into moving plates is called
   A. geography.
   B. absolute location.
   C. plate tectonics.
   D. the core.

____ **7.** Weathering is the
   A. study of climates.
   B. movement of glaciers.
   C. study of erosion.
   D. process of breaking down rock into smaller pieces.

____ **8.** What is one effect of chemical weathering?
   A. chemical changes in rocks
   B. formation of more ice
   C. loss of glaciers
   D. invention of sandpaper

____ **9.** What are the three main causes of erosion?
   A. fire, air, and movement
   B. water, wind, and glaciers
   C. volcanoes, earthquakes, and tornadoes
   D. rocks, soil, and sand

____ **10.** Lakes and valleys have been carved out by
   A. chemical weathering.
   B. wind.
   C. mountains.
   D. glaciers.

Climates and Ecosystems

SECTION 1 WEATHER AND CLIMATE

TEXT SUMMARY

Weather is the condition of the air in one place over a short period of time and is always changing. **Climate** is the kind of weather that an area has over a long period of time.

The sun is the source of the earth's climates. The earth moves around the sun in a yearly orbit, or path, which is called a **revolution**. Because the earth is tilted on its axis, sunlight hits different regions more directly at certain times of the year. This helps create seasons.

Latitude also affects climate. The sun's rays always fall most directly at or near the Equator. They are least direct near the North and South poles. As a result, most places near the Equator have warm climates while places farthest from the Equator are cold.

Prevailing winds, which occur in regular and predictable patterns, influence the climate of regions near them. Ocean currents, rivers of warm and cold water moving through the ocean, also affect climate.

Precipitation is all forms of water that fall to the earth's surface. The amount of precipitation a place receives has a major affect on its climate. Other influences on climate include elevation and nearby bodies of water and landforms.

The world can be divided into climate regions. Temperature and precipitation are used to classify climate regions.

THE BIG IDEA

Climate is the weather of an area over a long period of time. Location, latitude, elevation, and landforms influence climate.

GRAPHIC SUMMARY: Zones of Latitude and Prevailing Winds

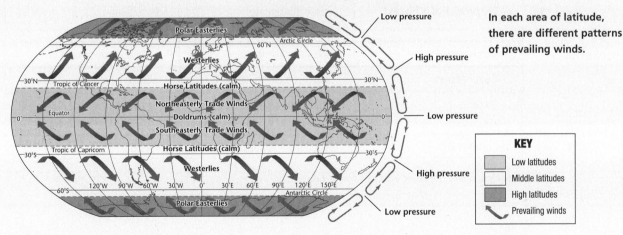

In each area of latitude, there are different patterns of prevailing winds.

KEY
- Low latitudes
- Middle latitudes
- High latitudes
- Prevailing winds

REVIEW QUESTIONS

1. Name three things that affect climate.

2. Map Skills In what directions do the prevailing winds move in the low latitudes?

ECOSYSTEMS

■ TEXT SUMMARY

An **ecosystem** is formed by the interaction of plant life, animal life, and the physical environment in which they live. The four ecosystems are forest, grassland, desert, and tundra. Geographers use the term **biome** to describe major types of ecosystems that can be found in various regions throughout the world.

Forest regions include many different types of biomes. A tropical rain forest has broadleaf evergreens, which keep their leaves all year. Rain forests grow where the temperature is warm and great amounts of rain fall. Forests of the middle latitudes consist mostly of broadleaf **deciduous** trees, which shed their leaves, usually in the fall. **Coniferous** forests may also grow in the colder parts of the middle latitudes and are named after the cones that protect their seeds. They have long, thin "needles" rather than broad, flat leaves. Most forests are a mixture of biomes. Another distinctive forest biome is **chaparral**, which includes small evergreen trees and low bushes, or shrub.

The characteristics of grasslands vary depending on their latitudes. Tropical grasslands, or **savannas**, grow in warm lands near the Equator. Temperate grasslands are found in cooler climates.

Desert ecosystems consist of plant and animal life that can survive with little water.

In **tundra** regions, temperatures are cool or cold. Plant life in this type of region survives in cold temperatures and short growing seasons and without sunlight for most of the winter.

> ### THE **BIG** IDEA
>
> There are four kinds of ecosystems. They are forest, grassland, desert, and tundra.

■ GRAPHIC SUMMARY: *Forest Biomes*

FOREST	LOCATION (EXAMPLE)	TYPE OF PLANTS
Tropical Rain Forest	near the Equator	broadleaf evergreens
Deciduous	Western Europe	broadleaf deciduous
Coniferous	northern North America	needle evergreens
Mixed	nothern United States	broadleaf deciduous and needle evergreens
Chaparral	southern California	low bushes

There are many different types of forest biomes.

■ REVIEW QUESTIONS

1. What are the four main ecosystems?

2. Chart Skills What kinds of plants are found in chaparral forests?

CHAPTER 2 *Test*

▪ IDENTIFYING MAIN IDEAS

Write the letter of the correct answer in the blank provided. (10 points each)

____ **1.** There are seasons because
  A. climate and weather are different.
  B. the earth is tilted on its axis.
  C. there are prevailing winds.
  D. the earth is round.

____ **2.** Where are the sun's rays most direct during all times of the year?
  A. near the North and South poles
  B. the Northern Hemisphere
  C. at or near the Equator
  D. the middle latitudes

____ **3.** Prevailing winds occur
  A. in regular and predictable patterns.
  B. during different seasons.
  C. only near the Equator.
  D. below the oceans.

____ **4.** Precipitation includes
  A. ocean currents, wind, rain.
  B. ocean currents, snow, rain.
  C. wind, rain, sleet.
  D. rain, snow, hail.

____ **5.** What two categories are used to classify climate regions?
  A. weather and latitude
  B. winds and ocean currents
  C. temperature and precipitation
  D. landforms and elevation

____ **6.** What is an ecosystem?
  A. the interaction of plant life, animal life, and the physical environment in which they live
  B. major types of plant life that can be found throughout the world
  C. a mix of similar groups of plants that naturally grow in one place and depend on one another
  D. the physical conditions of the natural surroundings

____ **7.** What is the most common type of tree in a mid-latitude forest?
  A. chaparral
  B. coniferous trees
  C. deciduous trees
  D. trees with small leaves or needles

____ **8.** Tropical grasslands
  A. grow near the Equator.
  B. include chaparral.
  C. grow in cool climates.
  D. are like ocean currents.

____ **9.** Desert ecosystems
  A. need a lot of water.
  B. need little water.
  C. include tropical forest.
  D. include coniferous trees.

____ **10.** Where are tundra ecosystems found?
  A. near the Equator
  B. in warm climates
  C. in cold climates
  D. in deciduous forests

Population and Culture

SECTION 1

THE STUDY OF HUMAN GEOGRAPHY

◼ TEXT SUMMARY

Human geography studies population and culture, as well as languages, religions, customs, and economic and political systems. **Culture** is made up of people's beliefs, actions, and way of life.

The world's population today is more than six billion. The population density in some places is much higher than in other places. **Population density** is the average number of people in a square mile or square kilometer.

The world's population has been growing very rapidly since the 1950s (see chart). This increase is not divided equally among countries or parts of countries. **Urbanization**, or the

growth of city populations, is happening throughout the world.

Differences in population are often the result of differences in cultures. Social organization is the way members of a culture organize themselves into groups. In all cultures the family is the most important part of social organization. Groups of people who speak the same language often share the same customs. Religion supports the values that a group of people believe are important.

Both internal and external influences affect a culture. **Cultural convergence** occurs when customs of a society come in contact with those of another culture. **Cultural divergence**, on the other hand, refers to the restriction of a culture from outside cultural influences.

THE **BIG** IDEA

Population is distributed unevenly over the world. During the twentieth century, the world's population grew more rapidly than ever before.

◼ GRAPHIC SUMMARY: *World Population Growth:*
A.D. *1150 to 2050*

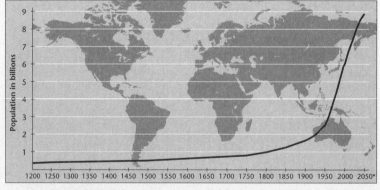

For many centuries, the world's population grew at about the same rate.

Source: United Nations Population Division
*Estimate

◼ REVIEW QUESTIONS

1. In what kinds of places would you expect to find the greatest population density?

2. **Graph Skills** What was the world's population in 1950?

POLITICAL AND ECONOMIC SYSTEMS

■ TEXT SUMMARY

There are about 200 independent countries in the world. Four ideas define a place as a country: clearly defined territory, population, sovereignty, and government. **Sovereignty** is freedom from outside control.

Countries have different government systems. A country with a central government that rules the entire nation has a **unitary** system. A **federation** refers to a country in which the national government shares power with state governments. In a **confederation**, smaller levels of government keep most of the power and give the central government very limited powers.

Governments differ in authority. In an **authoritarian** government, leaders hold all, or nearly all, political power. Today the most common form of authoritarian government is a **dictatorship**, in which a person or small group holds most power. Dictators usually take power by military force.

Throughout history, the most common type of authoritarian government has been a **monarchy**. Monarchs are hereditary rulers, such as kings and queens, who were born into the ruling family.

In a **democracy**, people elect their leaders. Most democracies have representative governments in which adult citizens can vote for people to make laws.

A country's economic system determines how goods and services are produced and distributed. In a **traditional economy**, all goods and services produced are consumed in the family or village,

leaving little surplus for trade. A **market economy** allows individuals or companies to make decisions concerning production and distribution. In a **command economy**, a central government controls the economic system.

THE **BIG** IDEA

Countries have different ways of organizing their governments and their economies.

■ GRAPHIC SUMMARY:
World Economic Systems

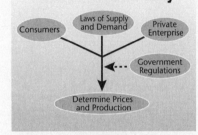

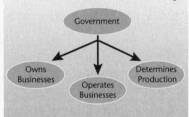

Each economic system has its own way of organizing economic activities.

■ REVIEW QUESTIONS

1. How is the way a monarch gets power different from the leader of a democratic country?

2. Diagram Skills In which economic system is the government most involved?

CHAPTER 3 *Test*

◼ IDENTIFYING MAIN IDEAS

Write the letter of the correct answer in the blank provided. (10 points each)

____ 1. Culture includes
   A. language, religion, and way of life.
   B. the houses a group of people build.
   C. a group's works of art.
   D. all the items a group of people make.

____ 2. What is population density?
   A. the people who live in the most crowded parts of cities
   B. the increase in the number of people from year to year
   C. all the people alive in the world today
   D. the average number of people in a square mile or square kilometer

____ 3. Which of the following statements is most accurate about the world's population growth?
   A. It has grown at a steady rate for the last 1,000 years.
   B. It is growing more slowly now than 100 years ago.
   C. It has grown more rapidly in the past 50 years than ever before.
   D. It is not taking place in cities.

____ 4. Urbanization is the
   A. decline of city populations.
   B. growth of country populations.
   C. growth of city populations.
   D. decline of country populations.

____ 5. What is the most important unit of social organization in all cultures?
   A. the family
   B. social class
   C. religion
   D. gender

____ 6. Which has the most power in a unitary system of government?
   A. the central government
   B. the state governments
   C. power is shared equally
   D. business owners

____ 7. Who holds the power in an authoritarian government?
   A. the people who vote
   B. all individuals
   C. the leader or leaders
   D. a group who must be elected

____ 8. Which statement is true for all democracies?
   A. They are all ruled by a dictator.
   B. The people elect the leaders.
   C. The leader holds all political power.
   D. They all have rulers who inherit power.

____ 9. Who makes decisions about producing goods and services in a market economy?
   A. The state makes all decisions.
   B. The state makes most decisions.
   C. Elected leaders make the decisions.
   D. Individuals or companies make the decisions.

____ 10. Which of the following statements is true about a traditional economy?
   A. The government controls the economy.
   B. The economy does not produce surplus goods for trade.
   C. It is a free enterprise system.
   D. Decisions are often made to achieve social or political goals.

Resources and Land Use

 **SECTION 1** *WORLD RESOURCES*

◾ TEXT SUMMARY

All people depend on **natural resources**, the materials that people take from the natural environment, for food, water, tools, and other needs. **Renewable resources** are those that the environment replaces. Sunlight, water, and soil are renewable resources.

Nonrenewable resources cannot be replaced once they are used. **Fossil fuels**, such as coal, oil, and natural gas, are nonrenewable. Many metals and other minerals cannot be replaced once they are used up. But objects made of them can be recycled so that the minerals can be used again.

Modern countries depend on energy from fossil fuels. Oil and natural gas are not spread out evenly around the world. Over half the world's known oil supply is in Southwest Asia. Coal is found in more places than oil or natural gas. But burning coal can cause air pollution.

Nuclear energy is produced by splitting uranium atoms to release their stored energy. Many people worry about leaks, explosions, and wastes from nuclear plants.

Many experts believe that countries must find renewable sources of energy. Water power uses the energy of falling water to create energy. **Geothermal energy** comes from the heat inside the earth. **Solar energy** is energy produced by the sun. It is not used much today, but it may provide the best source of energy for the future.

> **THE BIG IDEA**
>
> People use natural resources to survive and meet their other needs. Modern societies depend on reliable sources of energy.

◾ GRAPHIC SUMMARY: *Renewable and Nonrenewable Sources of Energy*

RENEWABLE ENERGY SOURCES

Water Power	Geothermal Energy	Solar Energy

NONRENEWABLE ENERGY SOURCES

Coal	Oil	Natural Gas

Energy sources that are renewable can be replaced.

◾ REVIEW QUESTIONS

1. How can recycling help with the problem of some nonrenewable resources?

2. Diagram Skills Why might a manufacturer prefer to depend on water power instead of oil?

WORLD ECONOMIC ACTIVITY

▣ TEXT SUMMARY

People acquire things needed to survive and luxuries they desire by earning a living. Geographers and economists classify these economic activities into four categories.

Primary economic activities rely directly upon natural resources, such as farming and mining. (See chart below.) Farming methods differ around the world. In less prosperous countries, farmers practice **subsistence farming**. They grow only enough for their own family or village. In countries with more advanced economies, farmers practice **commercial farming**. These farmers raise crops and animals to be sold for profit.

When people use raw materials to produce new products, such as processing wheat into flour, they are engaging in **secondary economic activities. Tertiary activities** refer to service indus-

tries, such as health care. **Quaternary economic activities** focus on the acquisition, processing, and sharing of information, as in education.

Nations establish trading networks when they do not have the resources and goods they want. The goods that are sent out of a country are called **exports**. The goods that are brought into a country are called **imports**.

Economic activities and trade patterns influence a country's level of development. Modern industrial societies are considered developed countries, whereas countries with lower levels of prosperity are considered underdeveloped. Nations showing evidence of progress are considered developing. One way to measure a country's level of development is to look at the per capita gross domestic product (GDP), the total value of goods and services produced in a country within a year divided by the total population.

> ### THE **BIG** IDEA
>
> Economic activities are the ways people earn their living. Countries are at different stages of economic development.

▣ GRAPHIC SUMMARY: *Four Levels of Economic Activities*

	PRIMARY ACTIVITIES	SECONDARY ACTIVITIES	TERTIARY ACTIVITIES	QUATERNARY ACTIVITIES
LINK TO NATURAL RESOURCES	• Use natural resources directly	• Process natural resources	• Do not directly gather or process raw materials	• Do not need to be located near resources or a market
EXAMPLES	• Farming • Fishing • Mining • Forestry	• Processing flour from wheat • Making lumber from trees • Producing electrical power	• Doctors • Salespeople • Firefighters • Truck drivers	• Education • Government • Information Processing • Research

Economic activities can be grouped by how and if they use natural resources.

▣ REVIEW QUESTIONS

1. How does subsistence farming differ from commercial farming?

2. Diagram Skills What type of economic activity is firefighting?

CHAPTER 4 *Test*

▨ IDENTIFYING MAIN IDEAS

Write the letter of the correct answer in the blank provided. (10 points each)

____ 1. What is a renewable resource?
   A. a resource that can never be used again
   B. a resource that cannot be used unless you pay for it
   C. a resource that the environment will replace
   D. a resource that comes from fossil fuel

____ 2. Which of the following forms of energy comes from fossil fuels?
   A. oil
   B. solar power
   C. geothermal energy
   D. water power

____ 3. What part of the world has over half the world's known oil supply?
   A. North America
   B. Western Europe
   C. Southern Africa
   D. Southwest Asia

____ 4. Why are countries trying to find alternatives to nonrenewable energy sources?
   A. Nations without nonrenewable sources want to put those with these sources out of business.
   B. Once nonrenewable sources are gone, there are no more sources of this energy.
   C. Once nonrenewable sources are depleted, they are very expensive to produce again.
   D. Nonrenewable sources will never be depleted, so there is no need for alternatives.

____ 5. What do you call energy that comes from the heat inside the earth?
   A. solar power
   B. nuclear energy
   C. geothermal energy
   D. fossil fuel

____ 6. What kind of economic activities are fishing and mining?
   A. tertiary activities
   B. primary activities
   C. secondary activities
   D. quaternary activities

____ 7. In which type of country would farmers most likely practice commercial farming?
   A. underdeveloped
   B. developing
   C. developed
   D. democratic

____ 8. Why do nations import from and export to other nations?
   A. to convince people to immigrate
   B. to fulfill an economic category
   C. to continue good relations
   D. to trade for the resources and goods they want

____ 9. What is per capita gross domestic product (GDP)?
   A. the salary a person earns each year
   B. the total value of goods and services produced in a country in a year divided by the total population
   C. all the products a country produces from raw materials
   D. each person's share of a country's products and services

____ 10. Who would use most of a subsistence farmer's crops?
   A. the farmer's family and village
   B. the people who buy the crops
   C. commercial farmers
   D. people around the world

Regional Atlas

INTRODUCTION TO THE UNITED STATES AND CANADA

■ TEXT SUMMARY

THE BIG IDEA

The United States and Canada are two vast nations that share most of North America. Both are wealthy, developed nations with rich natural resources.

Scientists believe that the first people to populate North America migrated from Asia and are known today as Native Americans. They were followed by the Europeans and Africans. English settlers established 13 **colonies**, territories separated from but subject to a ruling power. Eventually, the settlers broke ties with Great Britain to form the United States of America. Canada also ended ties with Great Britain to become a democracy.

The physical features of both nations include high mountain chains in the west, plains in the central area, and lower mountains in the east. The Rocky Mountains form the **continental divide**, a boundary that separates rivers flowing toward opposite sides of a continent. The variety of ecosystems includes arctic tundra, several types of forests, grasslands, and desert scrub. While Canada has a colder climate than the United States, both countries have climate differences between east and west.

The United States has over 275 million people, whereas Canada has approximately 31 million. At least three fourths of people in both countries live in urban areas. The **standard of living**, a measurement based on available education, housing, health care, and nutrition, is considered high in both nations. Americans and Canadians have long life expectancies and extensive education systems, which contribute to high rates of **literacy**, or the ability to read and write.

Technological development has made high-tech industries an influential part of both economies. The United States and Canada are two of the world's largest energy producers and consumers. Although the United States has an abundance of fossil fuels, it still must import energy, whereas Canada is self-sufficient in its energy needs.

■ GRAPHIC SUMMARY:
The United States and Canada

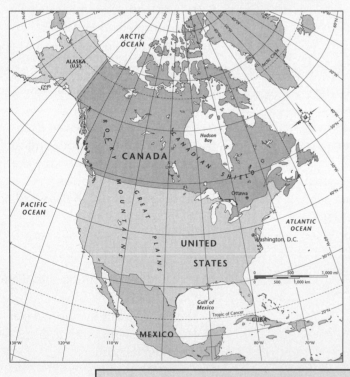

The United States and Canada cover most of North America.

■ REVIEW QUESTIONS

1. Name two features shared by the United States and Canada.

2. Map Skills Which oceans border the United States and Canada?

CHAPTER 5 *Test*

▣ IDENTIFYING MAIN IDEAS

Write the letter of the correct answer in the blank provided. (10 points each)

____ 1. Who were the first people to populate North America?
   A. Canadians
   B. Europeans
   C. Africans
   D. Native Americans

____ 2. Which term describes a territory separated from but subject to a ruling power?
   A. annex
   B. colony
   C. tributary
   D. striation

____ 3. Which physical feature is located in the central portions of both Canada and the United States?
   A. high mountain chains
   B. low mountains
   C. plains
   D. canyons

____ 4. What is the continental divide?
   A. a mountain in eastern North America
   B. a river system that includes the Great Lakes
   C. the Mississippi River
   D. a boundary that separates rivers flowing toward opposite sides of a continent

____ 5. Which statement does *not* describe the climates of the United States and Canada?
   A. Canada has a colder climate.
   B. Both countries have climate differences between east and west.
   C. Canada has a warmer climate.
   D. The United States has a warmer climate.

____ 6. What is the standard of living like in the United States and Canada?
   A. high in both countries
   B. much higher in the United States.
   C. much higher in Canada
   D. very low in both countries

____ 7. What factor most contributes to high rates of literacy in each nation?
   A. large populations
   B. good economies
   C. small populations
   D. extensive education systems

____ 8. What proportion of Americans and Canadians live in urban areas?
   A. one quarter
   B. three fourths
   C. one half
   D. nine tenths

____ 9. Which industry is an influential part of both economies?
   A. agricultural industries
   B. manufacturing industries
   C. service industries
   D. high-tech industries

____ 10. Which statement correctly describes energy production and consumption in these countries?
   A. Canada imports energy, whereas the United States is self-sufficient.
   B. The United States imports energy, whereas Canada is self-sufficient.
   C. Both countries are self-sufficient.
   D. Both countries import energy.

A Profile of the United States

SECTION 1 A RESOURCE-RICH NATION

▣ TEXT SUMMARY

The United States is the world's fourth largest country in area and the third largest in population. It has a higher **gross national product (GNP)** than any other country. GNP is the total value of goods and services that a country produces in a year.

One reason for the wealth of the United States is that it is rich in natural resources. Farmers grow crops on the country's rich soils. Forests supply lumber for housing, furniture, paper, and other products. Mineral resources include fossil fuels—coal, oil, and natural gas. Other mineral riches include copper gold, lead, titanium, uranium and zinc.

The United States built transportation systems to help move raw materials and finished products. In the 1800s, steamboats and canals made water routes faster and cheaper. Later, railroads, automobiles, and an interstate highway system improved travel over land.

Communications improved with the invention of the telegraph and telephone. Today people and businesses are communicating using computers, satellites, and other forms of **telecommunication**, or communication by electronic means.

The political system has also been vital to the economic success of the United States. It reflects one of the country's most important shared values—the belief in individual equality, opportunity, and freedom. These values are aided by an economic system of **free enterprise**, which lets individuals own, operate, and profit from their own businesses.

> ## THE **BIG** IDEA
>
> **Rich natural resources, hardworking people, a free-enterprise system, and systems of transportation and communications have led to the economic success of the United States.**

▣ GRAPHIC SUMMARY: *United States Economic Success*

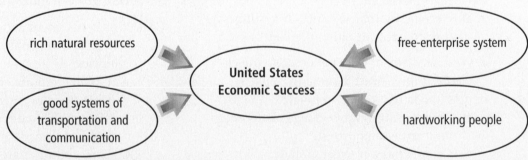

Many factors have led to the economic success of the United States.

▣ REVIEW QUESTIONS

1. Name three natural resources that have helped the United States to become wealthy.

2. **Diagram Skills** What four factors have contributed to the economic success of the United States?

SECTION 2 A NATION OF CITIES

■ TEXT SUMMARY

The United States is a nation of city dwellers. About 80 percent of the people live in **metropolitan areas**, cities and their suburbs.

The location of a city is important to its growth. But as the nation's economy changed, so did the factors that made a place a good location.

Transportation is one factor. The first U.S. cities were Atlantic Ocean ports, where goods were shipped to and from Europe. As settlers moved inland, they shipped their crops on rivers, and river cities grew. By the mid-1800s, cities were being built along the expanding railroads. Automobiles gave people more freedom of movement. Many people and businesses moved from cities to suburbs, areas on the outer edges of cities.

As transportation improved, people had more choices about where they would live and work. Many people moved to cities in the South and West, where winters are warmer than in the Northeast. Cities like New York and Chicago

remained important because of their many jobs and different activities.

Farms, towns, and cities all have a part in the nation's economy. Each depends on the others. There is a **hierarchy**, or ranking, of places according to their function. Smaller places serve a small area, while larger cities may serve the entire country and even much of the world.

THE BIG IDEA

U.S. cities have grown because of location, transportation, economy, and people's choices. Different-size cities have different purposes.

■ GRAPHIC SUMMARY:
Urban Hierarchy

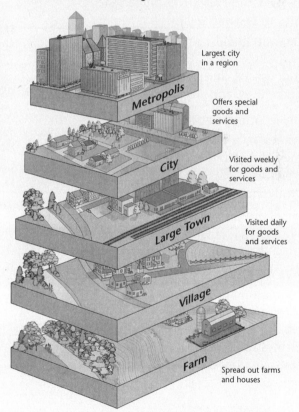

Largest city in a region

Metropolis — Offers special goods and services

City — Visited weekly for goods and services

Large Town — Visited daily for goods and services

Village

Farm — Spread out farms and houses

Each kind of place serves an important purpose in the urban hierarchy.

■ REVIEW QUESTIONS

1. Why did the first U.S. cities develop near the Atlantic Ocean?

2. Diagram Skills Which place serves the smallest area?

CHAPTER 6 *Test*

◼ IDENTIFYING MAIN IDEAS

Write the letter of the correct answer in the blank provided. (10 points each)

____ 1. Where does the United States rank among the nations in gross national product?
A. first
B. second
C. third
D. fourth

____ 2. Where does the United States rank among the nations in population?
A. first
B. second
C. third
D. fourth

____ 3. What kinds of natural resources helped the United States to become wealthy?
A. steamboats, railroads, and automobiles
B. telephones, telegraphs, and computers
C. farmland, forests, and minerals
D. canals, satellites, and electronics

____ 4. What are telecommunications?
A. written messages about phone calls
B. computers, telephones, and other electronic devices
C. television commercials
D. ads in magazines

____ 5. What is a free enterprise system?
A. a way that people can give away goods and services
B. a system in which there is no charge for transportation
C. a system in which the state controls all new businesses
D. a system that allows people to own and run their own businesses

____ 6. What is a metropolitan area?
A. a city that is growing
B. the area outside of a large city
C. a city that is part of another city
D. a large city together with its suburbs

____ 7. Where were the earliest U.S. cities located?
A. on Atlantic Ocean ports
B. on Pacific Ocean ports
C. near railroads
D. near rivers

____ 8. Which of the following is an example of personal choice in deciding where to build a home or business?
A. Shipping needs require the business to be on an ocean port.
B. People who like to swim set up a business in an area near a beach.
C. A hospital has nearby housing for its nurses.
D. A company told its employees they would have to move to a different factory.

____ 9. Which of the following is at the top of the urban hierarchy?
A. farm
B. large town
C. village
D. metropolis

____ 10. Which of the following helps make a location a good place for a city to grow?
A. a small population
B. nearby farms
C. poor transportation
D. good transportation

Regions of the United States

SECTION 1 THE NORTHEAST

◼ TEXT SUMMARY

The United States government divides the country into four major regions: the Northeast, South, Midwest, and West. The Northeast has fewer natural resources than the other regions. Its rocky soil and steep hills make farming difficult. Coal, found mainly in Pennsylvania, is its main mineral resource.

But the Northeast's waters have made it a center of trade, business, and industry. The North Atlantic Ocean is a rich source of fish. Excellent harbors helped ports to grow. The region's fast-flowing rivers provided power for early factories that made shoes, cloth, and other goods. River valleys became the routes for boats, wagons, railroads, and then highways. By the early 1900s, the Northeast was the world's most productive manufacturing region.

Cities on the Atlantic Ocean became international ports and shipbuilding centers. Population grew as people moved to the cities to work in new industries. Large numbers of European immigrants settled in the cities of the Northeast.

As cities grew they began to spread and run together. The far suburbs of one city reached to the suburbs of another. By the 1960s the area from Boston to Washington, D.C., became known as a **megalopolis**, or very large city made of several cities and their suburbs. Today about 40 million people, one seventh of the country's population, live in this megalopolis.

Some Northeast cities are losing population. As a result, city governments receive less in taxes and can provide fewer services.

THE **BIG** IDEA

Water helped the Northeast to grow, providing transportation routes, fishing grounds, and water power for industry. This region now has many cities and a high population density.

◼ GRAPHIC SUMMARY:
The Northeast

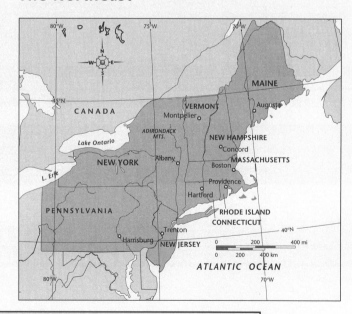

Many large cities are found in the states of the Northeast.

◼ REVIEW QUESTIONS

1. Name two ways that rivers were important in helping the Northeast to grow.

2. **Map Skills** Which seven states of the Northeast border the Atlantic Ocean?

THE SOUTH

◼ TEXT SUMMARY

The South includes the city of Washington, D.C., the nation's capital. The region is rich in resources and has become a popular place to live and work.

The South is warmer than other regions. It receives plenty of precipitation. Mixed forests grow in the warm, wet climate. The western part of the region, Oklahoma and western Texas, are semiarid.

Native Americans grew crops in the rich soil of the region. Some Europeans built huge plantations and used enslaved workers to grow tobacco, rice, and cotton. Farming is still important in the South.

Texas's oil industry began in 1901, and oil is still important to the region. Some of the largest oil reserves in the United States are located in the South. In the 1950s, new businesses began coming to the South. The space industry developed in Florida, Alabama, and Texas. Some businesses moved from the Northeast to take advantage of the South's lower land and labor costs.

Thousands of people moved to the South in search of jobs. The region's mild climate also helped it to attract tourists and retired people. The states of the South and West became known as the **Sunbelt.**

The South has a very diverse population. Among the region's major cities are New Orleans, Miami, Atlanta, Houston, Dallas, and Washington, D.C.

> ### THE **BIG** IDEA
>
> The South's warm climates and rich soils helped it prosper. Southern cities are growing rapidly as people move to the Sunbelt from other regions.

◼ GRAPHIC SUMMARY: *The South*

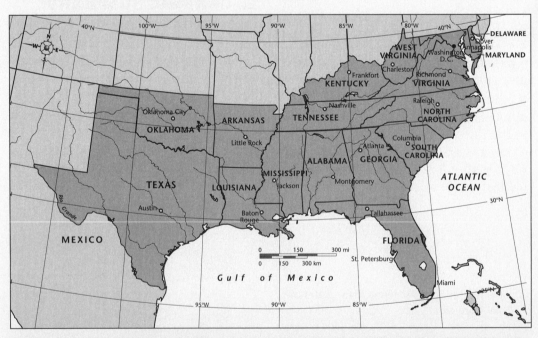

The South is bordered by both the Gulf of Mexico and the Atlantic Ocean.

◼ REVIEW QUESTIONS

1. What are two reasons for the South's rapid growth?

2. Map Skills Which states border the Gulf of Mexico?

THE MIDWEST

TEXT SUMMARY

The Midwest is often called "the nation's breadbasket" because the region's farms are among the most productive in the world. The export of farm products contributes to the wealth of the United States.

Differences in climate and soil affect farming. There are also differences in the **growing season**, the average number of days between the last frost of spring and the first frost of fall. The growing season in southern Kansas is more than 200 days, while near the Canadian border it is less than 120 days.

The warmer, wetter areas of Illinois, Indiana, and Iowa raise corn, soybeans, and hogs. In the drier Great Plains states to the west, farmers grow wheat, oats, and sunflowers. The cooler northern parts of the region produce hay and dairy cattle.

Technology has helped farmers grow more crops with fewer workers.

Business in many Midwestern cities and towns depends on farming. The Chicago Board of Trade is the largest **grain exchange**—a place where buyers and sellers make deals for grain.

Natural resources made the area a center of heavy manufacturing, oil and coal production, steel mills, and the auto industry. Water transportation helped industries and cities grow. Many large cities are on major rivers or the Great Lakes. The railroads also play an important part in shipping grain, livestock, and meat.

THE BIG IDEA

The climate and soil of the Midwest have made it a rich agricultural region. Industries grew because of transportation and natural resources.

GRAPHIC SUMMARY: *The Midwest*

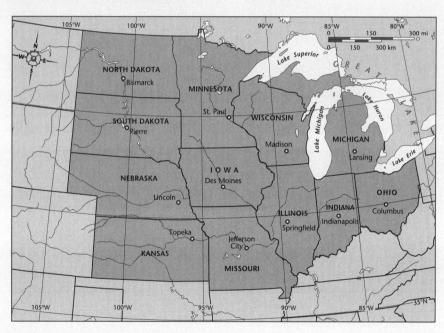

Four of the five Great Lakes are in the Midwest.

REVIEW QUESTIONS

1. Why is the Midwest called "the nation's breadbasket"?

2. **Map Skills** Which six states of the Midwest border the Great Lakes?

THE WEST

■ TEXT SUMMARY

THE **BIG** IDEA

The West's most outstanding feature is its landscape. The supply of water affects natural vegetation, economic activity, and where people live.

Water is the major factor affecting the West's natural resources, economic activity, and population density. Some areas have plenty of water, others have too little. Most of the region has either a semiarid or arid climate. Yet the western side of the mountains receives enough rain and has rich forests. Hawaii has a wet, tropical climate and tropical rain forests. Northern Alaska is mostly **tundra**, a cold, dry, treeless plain.

Gold, silver, uranium, and other minerals are found in the Rocky Mountains and in the Sierra Nevada. People once came to the region hoping to get rich by finding gold and silver. Others set up businesses to serve the miners. Oil and natural gas are also found in the region. Forestry and fishing are major industries.

Cities in the West grew when the first transcontinental railroad was completed across the country in 1869. Los Angeles, California, is now the second largest city, after New York, in the United States. To support its growing population, Los Angeles must bring in water through **aqueducts**, pipes that carry water over long distances.

Alaska is the largest state but has a small population. Some places can be reached only by boat or airplane. Hawaii, made up of many islands in the Pacific Ocean, is located more than 2,000 miles (3,218 km) from the United States mainland.

■ GRAPHIC SUMMARY:
The West

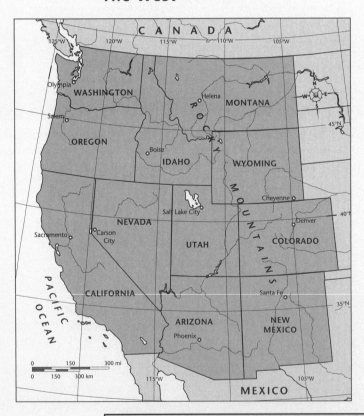

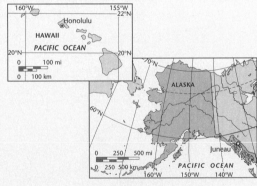

Mountains cover all the states in the West.

■ REVIEW QUESTIONS

1. How does Los Angeles provide enough water for its population?

2. Map Skills What ocean borders the West?

CHAPTER 7 *Test*

■ IDENTIFYING MAIN IDEAS

Write the letter of the correct answer in the blank provided. (10 points each)

____ 1. What helped the Northeast grow?
  A. gold, silver, uranium, and other minerals
  B. lots of good soil
  C. a semiarid climate
  D. water for transportation, fishing, and water power

____ 2. What is a megalopolis?
  A. a large city
  B. a small city with modern technology and good transportation
  C. several large cities and their suburbs, which run into one another
  D. several large cities that have poor populations

____ 3. Which two features helped the South to grow?
  A. good soil and a warm climate
  B. mineral wealth and a dry climate
  C. good soil and mountains
  D. warm climate and rich fishing areas

____ 4. What is a fairly new industry in the South?
  A. cotton farms
  B. the space industry
  C. cotton mills
  D. copper mining

____ 5. What is the Sunbelt?
  A. a region where people depend on solar power for energy
  B. the warm area of the South and the West
  C. a place where people study the sun's effect on the earth
  D. the part of the earth that gets the most sun all year

____ 6. Which statement is true of the Midwest's farms?
  A. They are some of the most productive farms in the world.
  B. They do not help the United States economy.
  C. They do not use up-to-date technology.
  D. Their main crop is cotton.

____ 7. What is a grain exchange?
  A. a place where grain is stored
  B. a farm where grain is grown
  C. a store where grain is sold
  D. a place where buyers and sellers make deals for grain

____ 8. What climate is most common in the West?
  A. wet and rainy
  B. arid or semiarid
  C. tundra
  D. tropical

____ 9. What factor in the West is most important in where people and businesses are located?
  A. the supply of water
  B. the supply of minerals
  C. forests
  D. the fishing industry

____ 10. What is an aqueduct?
  A. a good supply of anything
  B. an arid or semiarid region
  C. a pipe for carrying oil
  D. a pipe for carrying water long distances

Canada

REGIONS OF CANADA

◼ TEXT SUMMARY

Canada's ten **provinces** are similar to U.S. states, but with more power to govern themselves.

The four Atlantic provinces are called **maritime** provinces, meaning they border the sea. These small provinces are hilly, covered with forests, and have many good bays and inlets. The Grand Banks provide excellent fishing, but some areas have been overfished.

The heart of Canada's population and economy is in Ontario and Quebec, the Great Lakes–St. Lawrence area. It has three land areas: the Canadian Shield, with poor soil, a cold climate, and abundant minerals; the Hudson Bay Lowland, a wetlands between the Canadian Shield and Hudson Bay; and the St. Lawrence Lowlands, with rich soil, a mild climate, and sixty percent of Canada's population.

The three Prairie Provinces produce most of Canada's wheat and cattle. Oil and natural gas in Alberta provide wealth for the region. More than half the people in the Prairie Provinces live in cities, most of which lie along the railroads.

British Columbia has plenty of natural resources, including salmon, forests, and minerals. Vancouver, its largest city, is Canada's main Pacific port.

The northern area, 40 percent of Canada's land, has a harsh climate and rough land that make it hard to reach mineral wealth. The area includes the Yukon Territory, Northwest Territories, and as of 1999, Nunavut. This newest province was carved from the Northwest Territories as part of a land claim settlement with the native peoples.

> ## THE **BIG** IDEA
>
> Canada has five regions, rugged landscapes, and a cold climate. Quebec and Ontario are Canada's heartland.

◼ GRAPHIC SUMMARY:
Regions of Canada

Region	Province or Territory
Atlantic Provinces	New Brunswick
	Newfoundland
	Nova Scotia
	Prince Edward Island
Great Lakes and St. Lawrence Provinces	Ontario
	Quebec
Prairie Provinces	Alberta
	Manitoba
	Saskatchewan
British Columbia	British Columbia
Northern Territories	Northwest Territories
	Nunavut
	Yukon Territory

Canada has five distinct regions.

◼ REVIEW QUESTIONS

1. In which region do more than half of Canada's people live?

2. Chart Skills What are Canada's three Prairie Provinces?

THE SEARCH FOR A NATIONAL IDENTITY

◼ TEXT SUMMARY

Canada's lack of national unity mainly results from diversity among its people. Canada's history helps to explain this challenge of unity.

Many Canadians identify more strongly with regional and ethnic groups than with the nation. The Inuit and the Native Americans first populated the land when their ancestors migrated to North America thousands of years ago. The British and French arrived in the 1500s and began colonizing the region, devastating the native population with European diseases and warfare.

France and Britain battled over the land and fought four wars in North America. By 1763, France surrendered all of its land. French colonists were allowed to remain in Canada, and in 1774 the British government passed laws to ensure they would be able to maintain their own language, laws, and culture.

Britain continued to rule Canada directly until 1867. Then Canada was given its own government, but many decisions were still made by Britain. In 1931, Canada became a fully independent country. The government agreed to protect the rights of French-speaking citizens.

Although French and English are both official languages, only 15 percent of Canadians speak both. The majority of French-speakers live in the province of Quebec. French Canadians feel discriminated against, claiming they are denied jobs because they are of French descent. Many want Quebec to **secede**, or withdraw, from the rest of Canada. This movement, called **separatism**, would make Quebec an independent country.

Although most Canadians have British or French ancestors, there are many immigrants from other parts of Europe as well as from Asia.

> ### THE **BIG** IDEA
>
> Canadians have strong ties to their countries of origin, especially Britain and France. The government tries to encourage strong ties to Canada as well as diversity.

◼ GRAPHIC SUMMARY: *Ethnic Composition of Canada*

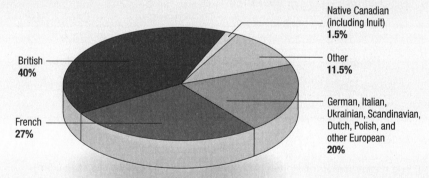

British 40%

French 27%

Native Canadian (including Inuit) 1.5%

Other 11.5%

German, Italian, Ukrainian, Scandinavian, Dutch, Polish, and other European 20%

Most Canadians trace their roots to the countries of Europe.

◼ REVIEW QUESTIONS

1. What do separatists in Quebec want?

2. **Graph Skills** What country in Europe is the original place of origin for most Canadians?

CANADA TODAY

◪ TEXT SUMMARY

Canada is a prosperous nation with a stable government and a high standard of living. Yet it faces many challenges.

THE **BIG** IDEA

Canada's size and location promote cooperation with the United States and the rest of the world. Yet Canada still faces the challenges of geography.

One challenge for Canada is extracting natural resources without harming the environment. Another challenge is urbanization. Today, 77 percent of the nation's population lives in cities. Canada must find a way to provide housing and services, control pollution, and prevent overcrowding in these urban areas.

Canada and the United States share the longest undefended border in the world. Travelers pay **customs**, or fees, to bring goods from one country to the other. These nations also connect on a cultural level. People living close to the border can enjoy radio and television programs from stations in both countries. Also, professional sports leagues include teams from both nations.

Another important link between Canada and the United States is economics. Canada buys nearly 25 percent of all U.S. exports, and the United States buys about 85 percent of Canadian exports. While these countries have many ties, Canadians consider the relationship uneven. Canadians are generally aware of events happening in the United States, while Americans tend to know little about Canada.

Canada's major ports on the Atlantic and Pacific oceans make it a major trading partner with many nations of the world. Canada has a special relationship with fellow member nations of the Commonwealth of Nations. Canada also works to keep peace in many parts of the world.

◪ GRAPHIC SUMMARY: *Comparing the United States and Canada*

Country	Population	Life Expectancy (years)	Per Capita GDP (in U.S. $)
Canada	30,675,398	79.2	$20,070
United States	270,311,758	76.1	33,900

Sources: *Microsoft Encarta Interactive World Atlas 2000* and *CIA World Factbook 2000*

The population of the United States is nearly nine times that of Canada. Both countries have a high standard of living.

◪ REVIEW QUESTIONS

1. What challenge does Canada face in developing its natural resources?

2. **Chart Skills** Which country has a higher per capita GDP?

CHAPTER 8 *Test*

◼ IDENTIFYING MAIN IDEAS

Write the letter of the correct answer in the blank provided. (10 points each)

____ **1.** What region has more than half of Canada's people?
  A. Atlantic Provinces
  B. Ontario and Quebec
  C. Prairie Provinces
  D. Northwest Territories

____ **2.** What does maritime mean?
  A. hilly and rocky
  B. covered with forests
  C. near the ocean
  D. small

____ **3.** Where do most of the people in the Prairie Provinces live?
  A. near the ocean
  B. on wheat farms
  C. on cattle ranches
  D. in cities

____ **4.** Why are many of Canada's minerals hard to reach?
  A. They are found in a harsh climate.
  B. Canada does not have machinery to remove them.
  C. The land is owned by Britain.
  D. Nobody knows where they are.

____ **5.** What happened to the French-speaking people after Britain defeated France?
  A. They had to leave the land.
  B. They could stay if they stopped speaking French.
  C. They could stay and keep their language and culture.
  D. They formed their own country.

____ **6.** What do separationists in Quebec want?
  A. to become an independent country
  B. to make English-speaking Canadians learn to speak French
  C. to have their own province
  D. to live in other parts of Canada

____ **7.** Which of the following is a challenge for Canada?
  A. trade with the world
  B. animal protection
  C. energy production
  D. urbanization

____ **8.** Why do Canadians consider their relationship with the United States uneven?
  A. Canada buys U.S. products, but the United States does not buy Canada's.
  B. Canadians must pay customs on U.S. goods, but Americans do not have to pay customs on Canadian goods.
  C. Canadians usually know more about the United States than U.S. citizens know about Canada.
  D. Canadian professional sports teams cannot compete against teams in the United States.

____ **9.** Which feature helps link Canada to the rest of the world?
  A. location of its major ports on both the Atlantic and the Pacific oceans
  B. its vast size
  C. its proximity to the United States
  D. its diverse population

____ **10.** What are customs on goods?
  A. the prices paid for goods
  B. labels that explain how to use goods
  C. an agreement that no taxes will be paid on goods from another country
  D. fees paid when goods are brought from one country to another

Regional Atlas

INTRODUCTION TO LATIN AMERICA

◼ TEXT SUMMARY

Native Americans formed the Inca, Aztec, and Mayan empires in Latin America. Explorers from Spain and Portugal conquered these complex societies and much of Latin America. As a result, many Latin Americans are **mestizos**, people of mixed Native American and European descent. Others are descendants of Africans who were brought to work as slaves on Latin American plantations.

In the 1700s and 1800s, Latin Americans fought for independence, which created republics but not democracy. In the 1900s, Latin Americans struggled for reform, eventually bringing about democratic governments and economic gains in a number of countries.

Mountains dominate much of Latin America, but the region also includes the **pampas**, grassy plains in southeastern South America. The Amazon rain forest is one of the largest ecosystems in the world. Islands, some of which are the tops of underwater mountains, are found in the Caribbean.

Atmospheric and ocean currents affect Latin America's climate. These currents can create **tropical storms**, with winds of at least 39 miles per hour. These can become **hurricanes**, with winds of at least 74 miles per hour, which devastate islands and coastal regions.

As in other parts of the world, three major economic systems are found in Latin America. A **market economy** allows economic decisions to be determined by supply and demand, while the government makes those decisions in a **command economy**. Under a **traditional economy**, families produce goods and services for their own use.

◼ GRAPHIC SUMMARY: *Latin America*

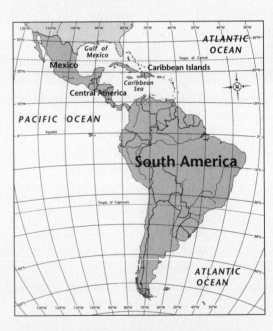

Latin America stretches from Mexico's northern border to the southern tip of South America.

> ## THE **BIG** IDEA
>
> Latin America includes Mexico, Central America, the Caribbean islands, and South America. The region has a variety of climates, landforms, and resources. All the countries were once European colonies.

◼ REVIEW QUESTIONS

1. What are the three different economic systems in Latin America?

2. **Map Skills** What bodies of water border Central America?

CHAPTER 9 *Test*

◨ IDENTIFYING MAIN IDEAS

Write the letter of the correct answer in the blank provided. (10 points each)

____ **1.** What geographic feature dominates Latin America?
  A. Amazon rain forest
  B. mountains
  C. pampas
  D. islands

____ **2.** Some Caribbean islands are
  A. the tops of underwater mountains.
  B. in the mountains.
  C. part of El Niño.
  D. near the Amazon River.

____ **3.** What is the pampas?
  A. the uppermost layer of a rain forest where tree branches meet
  B. the skeletons of tiny sea animals
  C. grassy plains in southeastern South America
  D. the lowland area drained by a river and its tributaries

____ **4.** Under what kind of economy does the government make all economic decisions?
  A. market economy
  B. traditional economy
  C. command economy
  D. democratic economy

____ **5.** Who were the first people to live in Latin America?
  A. Spanish
  B. Portuguese
  C. mestizos
  D. Native Americans

____ **6.** From which two countries did most Europeans come to Latin America?
  A. England and France
  B. Spain and Portugal
  C. Germany and Italy
  D. Belgium and Spain

____ **7.** What is a mestizo?
  A. a Latin American Indian
  B. a person who was born in Europe and lives in South America
  C. a person of mixed European and Native American descent
  D. a person whose ancestors came from Africa

____ **8.** What is a hurricane?
  A. a tropical storm with winds of only 10 miles per hour
  B. a warm water current in the Pacific Ocean
  C. a cold water current in the Atlantic Ocean
  D. a tropical storm with winds of at least 74 miles per hour

____ **9.** Who were brought to work as slaves on Latin American plantations?
  A. Amazonians
  B. mestizos
  C. Mexicans
  D. Africans

____ **10.** Which place is one of the largest ecosystems in the world?
  A. the Amazon rain forest
  B. the mountains of western South America
  C. Central America
  D. Mexico

CHAPTER 10

Mexico

 **SECTION 1** *GEOGRAPHY OF MEXICO*

■ TEXT SUMMARY

THE BIG IDEA

The central plateau is Mexico's heartland. Most of Mexico is mountainous. The coastal areas are different from the rest of the country.

Mountains dominate Mexico's geography. The Sierra Madre Occidental—the western Sierra Madre—is Mexico's largest mountain range. On the east, the Sierra Madre Oriental runs parallel to the eastern coast. The central plateau—the Plateau of Mexico—is Mexico's largest region and lies between the two mountain ranges. About four fifths of Mexico's people live on the plateau. It has large cities, rich farmland, and plenty of rain. Large numbers of people have moved to Mexico City in search of a better life.

Many active volcanoes border the southern edge of the central plateau. Earthquakes often shake the land, killing people and causing serious damage. Although the southern part of the central plateau is in the tropics, its climate is not tropical. That is because the plateau's high elevation keeps temperatures mild.

The plains of the northern Pacific coast are hot and dry. Farmers use **irrigation**, the artificial watering of farmland, to raise wheat, cotton, and other crops. By contrast, the Baja California **peninsula**, a strip of land sticking out into the ocean, is mostly mountainous desert.

Along the southern Pacific coast, mountains lie close to the ocean. The tropical climate and beautiful scenery have made tourism an important business. The Gulf coastal plain is rich in oil and natural gas. The Yucatán Peninsula is mostly flat. Ancient Mayan ruins attract tourists.

■ GRAPHIC SUMMARY:
Mexico: Political and Physical

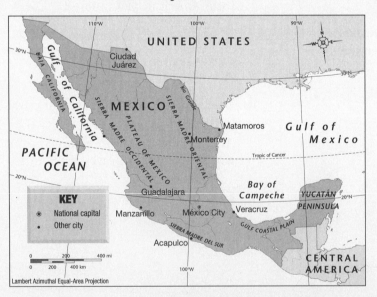

High mountains surround the central plateau, where four out of five Mexicans live.

■ REVIEW QUESTIONS

1. In what part of Mexico do most of its people live?

2. **Map Skills** What peninsula is in northwestern Mexico?

A PLACE OF THREE CULTURES

TEXT SUMMARY

The Aztecs built the most powerful empire in early Mexico. Spanish soldiers conquered the Aztecs in 1521. They built Mexico City on the ruins of the Aztec capital of Tenochtitlán. Mexico became part of the Spanish colony of New Spain.

In 1810, Miguel Hidalgo, a priest, began a rebellion against Spanish rule. Mexico won independence in 1821 but was ruled by military dictators.

After the Mexican Revolution, which lasted from 1910 to 1920, Mexico had a new constitution. It established a democratic republic. However, one political party held power until 2000.

The government bought land from large landowners and gave it to people who did not have any land. This policy is called **land redistribution**. Most of the reclaimed land is owned by the members of rural communities that practice subsistence farming. Approximately one third of Mexico's farms are huge commercial farms. They raise **cash crops**, farm crops grown for sale and profit.

Millions of Mexicans have no land and cannot find work. Many become **migrant workers** who travel from place to place where extra workers are needed to help grow and harvest crops.

Three quarters of Mexico's population live in urban areas. Most are very poor, although there is a growing middle class. Two of Mexico's most important industries are oil and tourism. Factories along the U.S. border assemble goods sold in the United States.

THE BIG IDEA

Three cultures—Indian, colonial Spanish, and modern Mexican—form Mexico today. Most Mexicans live in cities. Poverty is a problem in both cities and rural areas.

GRAPHIC SUMMARY: *The Three Cultures of Mexico*

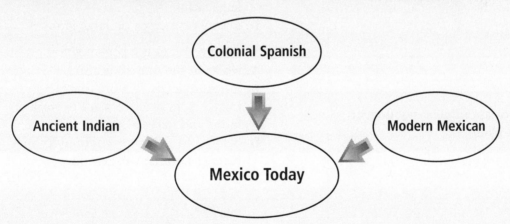

Three cultures have made Mexico what it is today.

REVIEW QUESTIONS

1. Name two of Mexico's most important industries.

2. **Diagram Skills** What are the three cultures that make up Mexico today?

CHAPTER 10 *Test*

◼ IDENTIFYING MAIN IDEAS

Write the letter of the correct answer in the blank provided. (10 points each)

_____ **1.** Most Mexicans live in
   A. the central plateau.
   B. the Sierra Madre Occidental.
   C. the Sierra Madre Oriental.
   D. Baja California.

_____ **2.** What keeps temperatures mild in Mexico's central plateau?
   A. irrigation
   B. elevation
   C. ocean breezes
   D. rain

_____ **3.** What makes the plains of the northern Pacific coast good for farming?
   A. It has a mild climate and plenty of rain.
   B. Farmers use irrigation to water the crops.
   C. Many rivers water the land.
   D. Farmers bring in soil from other parts of Mexico.

_____ **4.** An important industry in the southern Pacific coast is
   A. farming.
   B. oil.
   C. tourism.
   D. ranching.

_____ **5.** What is an important mineral resource in the Gulf coastal plain?
   A. gold
   B. tin
   C. coal
   D. oil

_____ **6.** What was New Spain?
   A. a part of Mexico
   B. a colony of Spain
   C. the Aztec capital city
   D. the Spanish capital city

_____ **7.** Until 2000, Mexico's government was controlled by
   A. the Aztecs.
   B. the Spanish.
   C. New Spain.
   D. one political party.

_____ **8.** What event made Mexico an independent country?
   A. the rebellion against Spain that began in 1810
   B. the Mexican Revolution that began in 1910
   C. the land distribution that gave land to landless farmers
   D. the conquest of the Aztecs

_____ **9.** What is land redistribution?
   A. planting new crops
   B. dividing large farms and giving land to people without land
   C. taking land from small farmers to create large farms
   D. raising cash crops on large farms

_____ **10.** A migrant worker is a person who
   A. works in the tourist industry.
   B. moves to a city to work in a factory.
   C. travels from place to place to work on farms and harvest crops.
   D. belongs to a farming community that practices subsistence farming.

Central America and the Caribbean

SECTION 1 CENTRAL AMERICA

 **TEXT SUMMARY**

Central America is an **isthmus**, a narrow strip of land connecting two larger land areas. The larger areas are the continents of North America and South America.

In 1914, the Panama Canal opened. It allowed ships to cross the isthmus and travel between the Atlantic and Pacific oceans. Ships no longer had to travel around the tip of South America.

Seven small countries make up Central America (see map). There are three major landforms—mountains, the Caribbean lowlands, and the Pacific coastal plain. Each region has a different climate. The rugged mountains, the core of the region, are difficult to cross and have caused transportation problems.

Central America's population includes Indians, Europeans (mostly Spanish), mestizos, and people of African descent. Most Central Americans are poor farmers with little political power. The wealthiest people, Europeans and mestizos, are mainly plantation owners. They dominate government in the region. There is a small but growing middle class.

Armed conflicts have been part of Central America's history. A shortage of farmland is one cause of unrest. Another cause is that governments mainly serve the interests of the wealthy. People opposed to those governments have sometimes organized **guerrilla** movements, armed forces outside the regular army. Guerrillas often fight in small bands against the government-controlled army. Cease-fires in several countries have brought hopes of peace.

> ### THE **BIG** IDEA
>
> Central America has many landscapes and climates. Most people are poor farmers, but power is held by a small number of very rich people. This has led to violent political conflicts.

GRAPHIC SUMMARY:
Central America

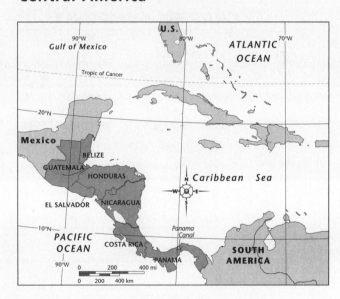

Central America is made up of seven small countries.

REVIEW QUESTIONS

1. What is the main occupation of most people in Central America?

2. Map Skills Which five countries of Central America border both the Pacific Ocean and the Caribbean Sea?

THE CARIBBEAN ISLANDS

◼ TEXT SUMMARY

The Caribbean islands are divided into three groups: the Greater Antilles, the Lesser Antilles, and the Bahamas. Most islands lie in the tropics.

The Bahamas form an **archipelago**, or group of islands. Most Lesser Antilles islands form another archipelago. The Greater Antilles includes the four largest islands—Cuba, Jamaica, Hispaniola, and Puerto Rico. Hispaniola is divided into two countries—Haiti and the Dominican Republic.

Mountainous islands are the tops of volcanic mountains. Some volcanoes are still active. The flatter islands are **coral islands**. They were created by the remains of tiny sea animals called coral polyps.

Sea and wind affect the climate. Ocean water keeps temperatures mild and humidity high. Winds affect the amount of rainfall. Islands that face the wind, or **windward** islands, get a lot of rain. The **leeward** islands face away from the winds and receive much less rain.

Many Caribbean people are descendants of Africans who were enslaved by European colonists and brought to work on plantations. Other people are descendants of immigrants from Asia who came after slavery ended. Many people are descended from Europeans or native Indians.

Many Caribbean people depend on farming. They grow sugar, bananas, coconuts, cocoa, rice, and cotton. Others work in industries related to farming, such as packaging rice products. The islands' beauty attracts tourists, but few islanders benefit from tourism. Many people leave the islands to find work or escape political unrest.

THE **BIG** IDEA

The Caribbean islands, located in the tropics, have three main island groups. Many people leave the islands to find work.

◼ GRAPHIC SUMMARY: *The Caribbean Islands*

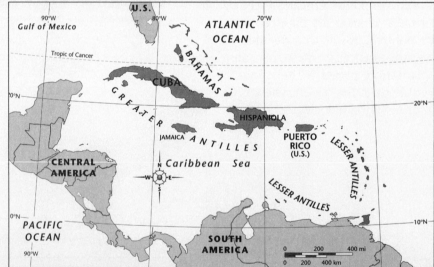

Many islands make up the Caribbean island region.

◼ REVIEW QUESTIONS

1. Which islands get more rain, windward islands or leeward islands?

2. **Map Skills** What bodies of water surround the Caribbean islands?

CHAPTER 11 *Test*

▨ IDENTIFYING MAIN IDEAS

Write the letter of the correct answer in the blank provided. (10 points each)

____ **1.** What is the name for a narrow strip of land that connects two larger land areas?
   A. canal
   B. isthmus
   C. mountains
   D. coastal plain

____ **2.** One cause of conflict in Central America has been
   A. too much farmland.
   B. democratic governments.
   C. a shortage of farmland.
   D. too few people.

____ **3.** The mountains of Central America
   A. are on the coasts.
   B. cause transportation problems.
   C. make transportation easy.
   D. are in only two countries.

____ **4.** Which sentence best describes most of the people of Central America?
   A. They are very poor farmers with little political power.
   B. They are wealthy people who own large plantations.
   C. They are members of a large middle class.
   D. They are members of the army.

____ **5.** What is a guerrilla?
   A. an animal found only in Central America
   B. a member of a government army
   C. a member of a group that fights against the army
   D. a wealthy owner of a Central American plantation

____ **6.** What is an archipelago?
   A. a group of islands
   B. any large island
   C. an island that receives a lot of rain
   D. an island that receives little rain

____ **7.** Which two countries make up the island of Hispaniola?
   A. Jamaica and Cuba
   B. Haiti and the Dominican Republic
   C. Puerto Rico and Jamaica
   D. Haiti and Jamaica

____ **8.** What kind of rainfall would you expect on the leeward side of an island?
   A. much more than on the windward side
   B. much less than on the windward side
   C. strong rains all the time
   D. no rainfall

____ **9.** After slavery ended in the Caribbean, many immigrants arrived from
   A. Africa.
   B. Asia.
   C. North America.
   D. Australia.

____ **10.** Why do many people in the Caribbean leave their islands?
   A. Island soil is not good for farming.
   B. Tourists use all the land.
   C. Volcanoes erupt too often.
   D. They leave to find work.

Brazil

SECTION 1 — THE LAND AND ITS REGIONS

▣ TEXT SUMMARY

THE BIG IDEA

Brazil is a giant country with nearly half of South America's people. The vast Amazon River basin is rich in plant and animal life.

Brazil has nearly half of South America's people and land. It has two main landforms—plains and plateaus. The huge Amazon River basin is a plains region. A narrow lowlands region follows the Atlantic coast.

A huge interior plateau drops sharply to the plains. The drop forms an **escarpment**, or steep cliff, between the two levels. The escarpment created a barrier to Brazil's interior for many years. Inland from the coast lies the *sertão*, or interior plateau.

Portuguese settlers started sugar plantations along the coast of the northeast in the 1500s. They brought enslaved Africans to do the work. Poverty in this region is great because the soil is poor and rain is uncertain.

Brazil's southeast is the smallest region and economic heartland. Many crops grow on its fertile soil. Coffee is the biggest and most important crop. About 40 percent of Brazilians live in this region, mostly in or near two cities—Rio de Janeiro and São Paulo. The cities attract poor people from rural areas who are looking for a better life. But many end up in slum communities called *favelas*. Houses there are often built of mud, tin, and wood boards.

Brazil's capital, Brasília, is in the Brazilian Highlands. It was built to attract people to this area, which is on the central plateau.

The Amazon River basin is home to thousands of kinds of plants and animals. Only about 10 percent of Brazilians live there, including about 200,000 Indians.

▣ GRAPHIC SUMMARY:
Brazil

Brazil is the largest country in South America and has many of the largest cities.

▣ REVIEW QUESTIONS

1. What region is Brazil's economic heartland?

2. **Map Skills** What city is located on the Amazon River?

BRAZIL'S QUEST FOR ECONOMIC GROWTH

■ TEXT SUMMARY

Brazil is a country of extremes. It is rich in natural resources but has much poverty. The country is taking steps to modernize its economy. The growth of industry has helped to create a middle class.

Many of the poorest Brazilians live in urban *favelas*. Others are small farmers who live in the northeastern *sertão*, a region with poor soil and uncertain rainfall.

To attack poverty, Brazil's government has increased industry and encouraged people to settle in the interior. The government has built steel mills, oil refineries, and hydroelectric dams. It built the new capital of Brasília in the Brazilian Highlands and built thousands of miles of new roads. To encourage people to move to the interior, the government gave away land and mining permits.

Manufacturing now makes up more than one third of Brazil's gross domestic product. The development of **gasohol**, a new fuel that mixes gasoline with ethanol, which comes from sugar cane, allows Brazil to grow its own fuel rather than import expensive foreign oil. About half of the people work in service industries such as hotels, restaurants, stores, and government.

Economic change has been good for Brazil, but it has had some unexpected bad effects. *Favelas* have grown larger as more people have moved to the cities. New settlers in the Amazon Basin cut down forests to plant crops. They learned, however, that the rain forest had kept the soil from washing away. Today the soil is no longer good for farming. **Deforestation**, or the permanent removal of woodland, threatens thousands of species of plants and animals in the Amazon. The government is now working to stop this threat.

> ### THE **BIG** IDEA
>
> Brazil is developing new industries and encouraging people to move to the interior to reduce poverty. Some development has hurt the environment.

■ GRAPHIC SUMMARY:
Percentage of Brazilians Living in Cities, 1974–2005

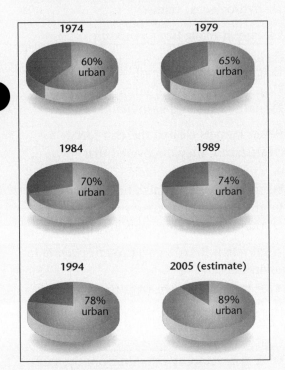

The percentage of Brazilians moving to cities has been increasing steadily.

■ REVIEW QUESTIONS

1. What has Brazil done to encourage the development of the country's interior region?

2. **Graph Skills** How did the percentage of people living in cities change from 1974 to 1994?

CHAPTER 12 *Test*

▣ IDENTIFYING MAIN IDEAS

Write the letter of the correct answer in the blank provided. (10 points each)

_____ **1.** What is an escarpment?
  A. an area of thick rain forest plants
  B. a river basin
  C. a sharp cliff between different levels of land
  D. a plateau area

_____ **2.** What was the main crop of Portuguese plantations in Brazil's northeast?
  A. coffee
  B. sugar
  C. cocoa
  D. rubber

_____ **3.** Which area of Brazil is its economic heartland?
  A. the Amazon River basin
  B. the Brazilian Highlands
  C. the northeast
  D. the southeast

_____ **4.** A home in a *favela* would probably be made of
  A. marble and glass.
  B. bricks and cement.
  C. steel bars.
  D. tin and mud.

_____ **5.** About how many Indians live in the Amazon river basin?
  A. 2,000
  B. 20,000
  C. 200,000
  D. 2,000,000

_____ **6.** To encourage people to move to the interior, Brazil built a new capital and
  A. many roads.
  B. railroads.
  C. rain forests.
  D. *favelas.*

_____ **7.** Another way the government encouraged people to move to the interior was by giving away
  A. land.
  B. free railroad tickets.
  C. a year's salary.
  D. hydroelectric dams.

_____ **8.** Gasohol is made from a mixture of
  A. gasoline and oil.
  B. gasoline and ethanol.
  C. natural gas and ethanol.
  D. natural gas and gasoline.

_____ **9.** When farmers cleared the rain forests to create farms, they discovered that
  A. crops grew very quickly.
  B. there were minerals under the soil.
  C. the soil was not good for farming.
  D. many kinds of animals ate their crops.

_____ **10.** What role is Brazil's government playing in deforestation?
  A. It is cutting down trees to grow crops.
  B. It is helping industries develop in the Amazon Basin.
  C. It is trying to stop it.
  D. It is developing ethanol from the trees that are being removed.

Countries of South America

 **SECTION 1** *THE NORTHERN TROPICS*

■ TEXT SUMMARY

The northern tropics, the five countries on the northern coast of South America, have both similarities and differences. Guyana, Suriname, and French Guiana together are called the Guianas. They share a tropical wet climate and a narrow coastal plain on the Atlantic Ocean. Their cultures are different from most of the rest of South America.

Many people in the Guianas are of Asian or African descent. Many others are **mulattoes**, people of mixed African and other ancestry. Most live by fishing or growing sugar cane and rice. Others mine **bauxite**, a mineral used in making aluminum.

Colombia and Venezuela have three physical regions—lowlands, mountains, and the **llanos**, or grassy plains. Climate depends on elevation. Different crops are grown at different elevations. (See diagram on right.)

Venezuela's economy is based on oil. Although Venezuela has huge oil reserves, oil is not a renewable resource. Therefore,

Venezuela is also investing in other industries, including bauxite and iron mines, power plants, and factories.

Colombia's farmers depend mostly on one crop—coffee. A country that depends on one crop, such as coffee, faces problems if prices drop or coffee trees die. The government is trying to encourage the export of other crops. Colombia also grows two illegal crops—marijuana and cocaine. People who control the drug trade have a lot of power. Colombia and the United States are working to end the drug trade and its violence.

THE **BIG** IDEA

There are five countries to the north of Brazil. Each one has its own economy and its own mix of people.

■ GRAPHIC SUMMARY:
Vertical Climate Zones in Latin America

Climate changes with the elevation of the land. Some crops grow best at certain altitudes.

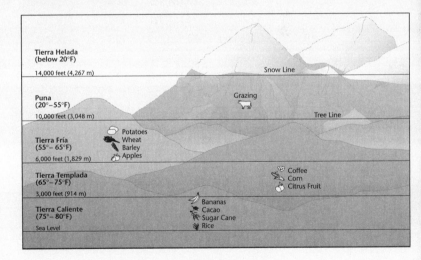

■ REVIEW QUESTIONS

1. Which country in the northern tropics is rich in oil?

2. Diagram Skills What is the name for the climate zone where coffee is grown?

THE ANDEAN COUNTRIES

■ TEXT SUMMARY

The Andes form the backbone of South America, shaping the economies and lifestyles of the people in Ecuador, Peru, Bolivia, and Chile. It is the longest unbroken mountain chain in the world.

The Andes stretch from the Caribbean Sea to the southern tip of South America. A long narrow coastal plain lies between the Andes and the Pacific Ocean.

In northern Chile, the coastal plain is occupied by the Atacama Desert, the driest place on earth. Between the peaks of the Andes are highland valleys and plateaus.

The climate in the Andes varies with elevation. At high elevations, only cold-weather plants grow. At the bottom of the eastern slopes are forested tropical lowlands called the *selva*.

People are drawn to the Andes because of its rich soil and wealth of minerals. The original inhabitants of the highlands were groups of Native Americans, who still make up between 25 and 55 percent of the populations of Bolivia, Ecuador, and Peru. These Indians follow a traditional lifestyle in the highlands, practicing subsistence agriculture.

The next largest group of inhabitants is mestizos, who speak Spanish and live in cities and towns. People of European background make up a small percentage of the population, but because they control most of the wealth, they have the most political power.

Chile is a long, narrow country and unlike other Andean nations, it has relatively few Indians. About two thirds of its people are mestizos. Another quarter is of European descent. Most Chileans live in the fertile Central Valley.

■ GRAPHIC SUMMARY:
The Countries of South America

Country	Population	Life Expectancy (years)	Per Capita GDP (in US $)
Argentina	36,265,463	74.5	9,110
Bolivia	7,826,352	60.9	1,030
Brazil	169,806,557	64.4	5,010
Chile	14,787,781	75.2	5,270
Colombia	38,580,949	70.1	2,390
Ecuador	12,336,572	71.8	1,660
Guyana	707,954	62.3	920
Paraguay	5,291,020	72.2	2,000
Peru	26,111,110	70.0	2,620
Suriname	427,980	70.6	820
Uruguay	3,284,841	75.5	6,110
Venezuela	22,803,409	72.7	3,840

Source: *Microsoft Encarta Interactive World Atlas 2000*

The Andean countries vary greatly in population size and in GDP.

■ REVIEW QUESTIONS

1. Which of the Andean countries has the smallest Indian population?

2. **Chart Skills** Which of the Andean countries has the smallest population?

THE SOUTHERN GRASSLAND COUNTRIES

▣ TEXT SUMMARY

The three nations of southern South America are Uruguay, Paraguay, and Argentina. They are among the richest countries of the continent. The region is bound together by several large rivers that flow into the Río de la Plata. The Plata is an **estuary**, a broad river mouth formed where a flooded river valley meets the sea.

The highest peaks of the Andes are in western Argentina. Lower down is the gently rolling **piedmont**, or foothills, region. The Gran Chaco is a hot, interior lowland in parts of Paraguay, Argentina, and Bolivia.

The **pampas** are temperate grasslands in Argentina and Uruguay. **Gauchos**, or cowboys, once herded cattle on the pampas. Now grains are grown there too. South of the pampas is Patagonia, a dry,

old plateau. It has oil and bauxite and is good for raising sheep.

Paraguay has no seacoast, but the Río de la Plata provides an outlet to the Atlantic Ocean. Most Paraguayans are mestizos. Paraguay and Brazil worked together to build the Itaipu Dam, one of the world's largest hydroelectric projects.

Uruguay has good grasslands for raising livestock. The country produces wool, meat, and leather. Most of the people of Uruguay and Argentina are of European descent.

Argentina is the wealthiest country in South America. Most Argentineans live in cities. There are many factories and good harbors.

> ### THE **BIG** IDEA
>
> Several large rivers link the three nations of southern South America. Argentina and Uruguay are among the richest countries in South America.

▣ GRAPHIC SUMMARY: Some Land Regions in Southern South America

Region	Location	Description
Piedmont	western Argentina	low, gently sloping foothills
Gran Chaco	Paraguay, Argentina, Bolivia	hot, interior lowland
Pampas	Argentina, Uruguay	temperate grasslands
Patagonia	southern tip of Argentina and Chile	cold and dry plateau

The countries of southern South America have some special land regions.

▣ REVIEW QUESTIONS

1. What is the wealthiest country of South America?

2. **Chart Skills** In what countries is the Gran Chaco located?

CHAPTER 13 *Test*

◼ IDENTIFYING MAIN IDEAS

Write the letter of the correct answer in the blank provided. (10 points each)

____ 1. How is the population of the Guianas different from other countries in Latin America?
   A. Most people in the Guianas are Native Americans.
   B. About half the people in the Guianas are of European descent.
   C. Almost all the people in the Guianas are of African descent.
   D. The Guianas have many people of Asian descent.

____ 2. What is bauxite?
   A. a form of silver
   B. a mineral used to make aluminum
   C. an oil rig
   D. an area good for ranching

____ 3. What does the word llano mean?
   A. a wide plain
   B. an oil drill
   C. a factory
   D. a hydroelectric plant

____ 4. Why is it a problem for Colombia's economy to depend on coffee?
   A. People will not work on coffee farms.
   B. If the price of coffee drops, Colombia will make less money.
   C. If the price of coffee rises, Colombia will make less money.
   D. People who sell drugs will not buy coffee.

____ 5. The Atacama Desert is
   A. in the rain forest.
   B. on the Atlantic coast.
   C. part of the coastal plain.
   D. high in the Andes.

____ 6. How do most Indians make their living in the Andean countries?
   A. They work in factories.
   B. They are government leaders.
   C. They are subsistence farmers.
   D. They own large farms.

____ 7. In which Andean country are two thirds of the people mestizos?
   A. Chile
   B. Bolivia
   C. Ecuador
   D. Peru

____ 8. How have the pampas changed?
   A. Gauchos set up more ranches than ever before.
   B. People built many large cities on the pampas.
   C. Farmers are no longer using the pampas to grow wheat.
   D. The pampas are now also used for growing grains.

____ 9. Which of the following is an estuary?
   A. Pampas
   B. Patagonia
   C. Río de la Plata
   D. Piedmont

____ 10. The Gran Chaco is
   A. a dry, cold plateau.
   B. a hot, interior lowland.
   C. a foothills region.
   D. a broad river mouth.

Regional Atlas

INTRODUCTION TO WESTERN EUROPE

◼ TEXT SUMMARY

Migration and the process of **cultural diffusion**, in which peoples adopt the practices of their neighbors, have affected the history of Western Europe.

Western Europe contains a variety of physical features. Oceans and seas surround much of Western Europe, while the **summits**, or highest points, of the Alps contrast with the flat North European Plain.

Temperate climates are caused by this region's proximity to the sea. The North Atlantic Drift, along with winds known as the **prevailing westerlies**, creates milder climates than those of other regions located at the same latitudes. The varying altitudes throughout Europe affect the vegetation and animal life of a region.

Western Europe occupies only 3 percent of the world's landmass, but it is one of the most densely populated regions in the world. Economic growth

has encouraged people to migrate to Western Europe from all over the world in search of employment.

The growing use of machines during the 1800s became known as the **Industrial Revolution**. Industrialization and many natural resources helped transform this region from an agricultural society to an industrial society.

In the 1950s, six Western European nations formed a "common market" for their mutual economic benefit. As it expanded, it became the European Union (EU). In 1999, this union introduced the **euro**, a single currency to be used by member nations.

The idea of free nationwide education originated in Europe. In all Western European nations, education is **compulsory**, or required, for a certain number of years.

THE BIG IDEA

The countries of Western Europe are home to many cultures. The region is small but densely populated and its economy is based on industry and services.

◼ GRAPHIC SUMMARY:
Migration to Europe

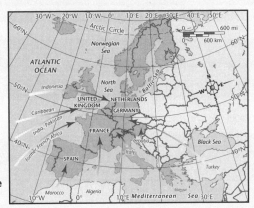

People migrate to Western Europe from all regions of the world.

◼ REVIEW QUESTIONS

1. Why is Western Europe one of the most densely populated regions in the world?

2. **Map Skills** According to the map, to which Western European country have Turkish citizens migrated?

CHAPTER 14 *Test*

◼ IDENTIFYING MAIN IDEAS

Write the letter of the correct answer in the blank provided. (10 points each)

____ **1.** The process in which peoples adopt the practices of their neighbors is called
    A. cultural diffusion.
    B. Industrial Revolution.
    C. Renaissance.
    D. migration.

____ **2.** Which physical feature surrounds much of Western Europe?
    A. the Alps
    B. oceans and seas
    C. the Northern European Plain
    D. rivers

____ **3.** How does Western Europe's proximity to the sea affect this region's climate?
    A. It makes the region prone to hurricanes.
    B. It makes the climate mild.
    C. It makes the region prone to tsunamis.
    D. It makes the climate very cold.

____ **4.** The highest point of a mountain is called a
    A. summit.
    B. peak.
    C. slope.
    D. base.

____ **5.** What is the euro?
    A. another name given for Western European nations
    B. the period when people migrated to Western Europe
    C. a common market between countries
    D. a single currency used by European Union member nations

____ **6.** Which of the following have affected Western Europe's ecosystem?
    A. climate and history
    B. economic activities
    C. human influence and varying altitudes
    D. migration and cultural diffusion

____ **7.** Western Europe occupies how much of the world's landmass?
    A. 97 percent
    B. 3 percent
    C. 15 percent
    D. 54 percent

____ **8.** Which of the following has encouraged people to migrate to Western Europe in search of employment opportunities?
    A. economic growth
    B. the Industrial Revolution
    C. the formation of the European Union
    D. the strong agricultural industry

____ **9.** The European Union was formed by
    A. companies that do business in Western Europe.
    B. people who work in factories in Western Europe.
    C. all the countries in Europe.
    D. six Western European nations that wanted a "common market" for their mutual economic benefit.

____ **10.** A compulsory education is an education that is
    A. for people who want to pursue a profession in science.
    B. required for a certain number of years.
    C. based on mathematics.
    D. for students who want to learn fine arts.

The British Isles and Nordic Nations

SECTION 1 *ENGLAND*

▣ TEXT SUMMARY

Great Britain is a large island that includes England, Scotland, and Wales. Together with Northern Ireland, they form the United Kingdom. Most people in the United Kingdom live in England.

England's Highlands are in the west. Land there is difficult to farm. The Midlands, once rich in coal, are the center of industry. The soil in the Lowlands is **fertile**, able to produce many crops. Lowland farms grow wheat and vegetables and raise sheep and cattle.

England's most important city is London. It is located on the Thames River. London is inland, but ocean ships can sail up the river.

The Industrial Revolution began in England. Factories first used water power to make cloth. Later they switched to coal as a source of power. England had major coal fields. It also had large amounts of iron **ore**, or rock containing a valuable mineral. The coal and iron were used to make steel.

The Industrial Revolution made Britain rich. It also made factory towns noisy and dirty. Britain led the world in industry until the late 1800s. Then, the United States and Germany began producing as much steel as Britain.

Much of Britain's coal is now gone. Today the country uses oil and natural gas found under the North Sea. Service industries are more important than factories. Britain's economy has been growing steadily.

THE **BIG** IDEA

Great Britain has been a center of trade and transportation. The Industrial Revolution began in Great Britain.

▣ GRAPHIC SUMMARY:
The British Isles

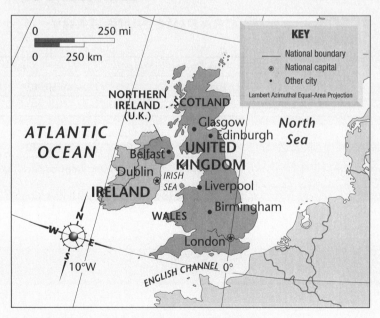

The British Isles include two large islands—Great Britain and Ireland.

▣ REVIEW QUESTIONS

1. What part of England is a center of industry?

2. Map Skills What places make up the United Kingdom?

SCOTLAND AND WALES

■ TEXT SUMMARY

Scotland was a separate country until it was united with England in 1707. It still keeps its own systems of law and education. Many Scots belong to the Presbyterian Church instead of the Church of England.

The Highlands region of Scotland is a large, high plateau with many lakes. Much of the Highlands are also covered with **moors**, plains with no trees. The moors have many **bogs**, areas of wet, spongy ground. Fishing and sheepherding are important industries in the Highlands.

Most of Scotland's people live in the Central Lowlands. In the 1800s, it was a center of industry. However, since the mid-1900s, many factories have closed and jobs were lost.

The Southern Uplands is close to Scotland's border with England. It is a sheep-raising region with many woolen mills.

Today, new industries are becoming important in Scotland. The discovery of oil in the North Sea brought new jobs. Computer and electronic businesses also have developed in some areas.

Wales has been united with England since 1284. Most of the Welsh people speak English, but many also speak Welsh.

Some of Great Britain's biggest coal mines are in Wales. By the mid-1900s, many mines and factories had to close because they were not modern. In the 1990s, new high-tech industries and tourism helped rebuild the economy of Wales.

> ### THE **BIG** IDEA
>
> Scotland and Wales have their own cultures, which are different from England's. Each is divided into highlands and lowlands.

■ GRAPHIC SUMMARY: *The United Kingdom*

The United Kingdom	Area (sq. mi.)	Population	Largest City
England	50,302	49,807,082	London
Northern Ireland	5,452	1,663,300	Belfast
Scotland	30,418	5,111,000	Glasgow
Wales	8,019	2,927,000	Cardiff

Source: The World Almanac and Book of Facts 2001

England is the largest part of the United Kingdom.

■ REVIEW QUESTIONS

1. Where do most people live in Scotland?

2. Chart Skills Which part of the United Kingdom has the second largest population?

THE TWO IRELANDS

◼ TEXT SUMMARY

Ireland is divided into Northern Ireland, which is part of the United Kingdom, and the Republic of Ireland, an independent country. Ireland's people are also divided by religion and culture.

The island's moist, marine climate keeps vegetation green. About one sixth of the land is covered by **peat**, a spongy material containing mosses and plants. Peat is used for fuel.

Invasions and war have shaped Ireland's history. Celtic tribes arrived first. They often defended themselves against Viking raids. After Normans from France conquered England in 1066, some took land in Ireland and forbade the use of Gaelic, the Celtic language. Eventually, English rulers began considering Ireland a possession of England.

In the 1500s, groups in Europe began a movement known as the Reformation, which led to a split from the Roman Catholic Church. Most English people became Protestants, whereas the Irish remained mostly Catholics. Conflict between Irish Protestants and Catholics led to **cultural divergence**, or deliberate efforts to keep the cultures separate.

In the 1840s, a plant disease known as a **blight** caused the Irish Potato Famine. The famine caused many deaths and resulted in anti-British feelings and immigration to the United States.

Many Irish wanted independence. After rebellions between 1916 and 1921, Ireland was divided into two parts. The six northeastern counties remained part of the United Kingdom. The rest eventually became independent as the Republic of Ireland in 1949.

A slight majority in Northern Ireland are Protestant. Most Catholics want to reunite all of Ireland, while most Protestants do not. Both sides have used violence. Steps toward peace began in 1994.

> ### THE **BIG** IDEA
>
> **Ireland is an island that is divided into two political regions: Northern Ireland and the Republic of Ireland. The two parts share a history of conflicts.**

◼ GRAPHIC SUMMARY: *Events in Ireland in the 1900s*

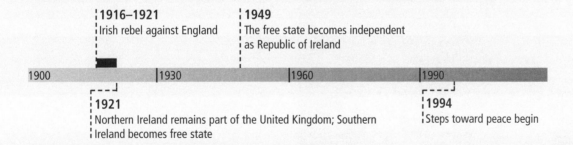

1916–1921
Irish rebel against England

1949
The free state becomes independent as Republic of Ireland

1900   1930   1960   1990

1921
Northern Ireland remains part of the United Kingdom; Southern Ireland becomes free state

1994
Steps toward peace begin

Ireland saw many changes in the 1900s.

◼ REVIEW QUESTIONS

1. What religions divide the people of Ireland?

2. Time Line Skills In what year did the Republic of Ireland become independent?

THE NORDIC NATIONS

TEXT SUMMARY

The Nordic nations are Norway, Sweden, Finland, Denmark, and Iceland. All are located in the northern latitudes. The region has many peninsulas and islands. Landforms vary greatly. Denmark is very flat, while Norway is very mountainous.

The Scandinavian Peninsula includes most of Norway and Sweden. Its coasts have flooded valleys called **fjords** that were carved out by glaciers. Most fjords have steep walls. Some are so deep that ocean-going ships can sail into them.

Volcanoes and glaciers exist side by side in Iceland. Icelanders use **geothermal energy**, created by the heat inside the earth, to produce heat and electricity.

Location in the northern latitudes results in long winters and short summers. In midwinter, the sun shines only two or three hours a day. In midsummer, the sun shines more than 20 hours a day.

Much of the Nordic region has a surprisingly mild climate. Warm ocean currents keep the coasts free of ice. Mountains in Norway block the warm air, however, making areas east of the mountains cold and dry.

The Nordic nations have similar histories. Vikings sailed out of the region from 800 to 1050. The nations were often united. Except for Finnish, the languages of these countries have common roots. Most of the people belong to the Lutheran Church.

The Nordic countries all have strong **mixed economies**. That means the government operates some businesses, and private companies operate others.

THE **BIG** IDEA

The five Nordic nations of northern Europe are united as a region by location and similar cultures.

GRAPHIC SUMMARY:
The Nordic Nations

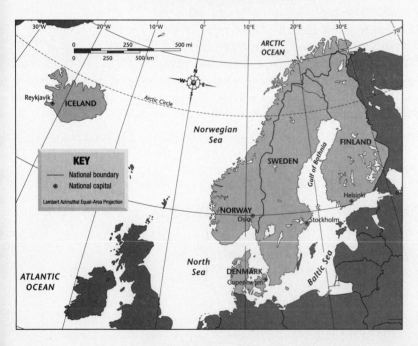

The Nordic nations share peninsulas and islands.

REVIEW QUESTIONS

1. What is a mixed economy?

2. **Map Skills** Which three Nordic nations have land that lies north of the Arctic Circle?

CHAPTER 15 *Test*

■ IDENTIFYING MAIN IDEAS

Write the letter of the correct answer in the blank provided. (10 points each)

_____ 1. What area is part of the United Kingdom but is not part of Great Britain?
   A. Scotland and Wales
   B. Northern Ireland
   C. the Republic of Ireland
   D. all of Ireland

_____ 2. Where did the Industrial Revolution begin?
   A. the United States
   B. Germany
   C. England
   D. Ireland

_____ 3. What is a moor?
   A. wet, spongy ground
   B. a plain with no trees
   C. moss used for fuel
   D. good farmland

_____ 4. Where do most people in Scotland live?
   A. the Central Lowlands
   B. the Southern Uplands
   C. the Highlands
   D. near the North Sea

_____ 5. Why did many factories in Wales close in the mid-1900s?
   A. They were not modern enough.
   B. There was no need for factory goods.
   C. Tourism forced the factories to close.
   D. There was no coal to power them.

_____ 6. What is the main use for peat?
   A. food
   B. fertilizer for crops
   C. fuel
   D. keeping the land green

_____ 7. What is included in Northern Ireland?
   A. the Republic of Ireland
   B. six counties that are part of the United Kingdom
   C. six counties that are part of the Republic of Ireland
   D. the independent part of Ireland

_____ 8. Which of the following explains what makes the Nordic nations a region?
   A. They are located in the northern latitudes.
   B. They are located in Europe.
   C. All the people speak Finnish.
   D. All the people belong to the Catholic Church.

_____ 9. What is a fjord?
   A. a steep mountain
   B. a long summer day with sun for more than 20 hours
   C. a flooded valley with steep sides
   D. a warm ocean current that keeps the climate mild

_____ 10. The Nordic nations all have
   A. summer all year.
   B. moors.
   C. winter all year.
   D. mixed economies.

CHAPTER 16

Central Western Europe

SECTION 1 *FRANCE*

■ TEXT SUMMARY

THE BIG IDEA

France has a distinct identity based on its history, language, and culture. It also has a variety of physical and economic regions.

Although France has a strong national identity, the people of each region have their own traditions and way of life. The Paris Basin in the north is the center of France's main manufacturing center. Paris, the capital city, is its center. The southwest is famous for wine grapes. Bordeaux is its main city.

In southern France, the Rhône River flows between two mountain areas. The Massif Central is west of the Rhône. The snow-covered Alps separate France from Italy. In 1965, a tunnel was built through the mountains.

Between the Alps and the Mediterranean Sea is a coastal land called the French Riviera. Its beautiful beaches attract many tourists. Marseille is the busiest seaport in France and the second busiest in Western Europe. The Rhine River, in eastern France, forms part of France's border with Germany. This region has large deposits of iron ore and coal.

For hundreds of years, France was ruled by kings. In 1789, the French Revolution ended the monarchy. Since then, France has had many forms of government. The French language helps to unify the French people. The French are proud of their philosophers and artists.

France is a wealthy nation but has faced some economic problems. A **recession**, or long decline in business activity, caused many people to lose their jobs in the 1990s.

■ GRAPHIC SUMMARY:
Central Western Europe

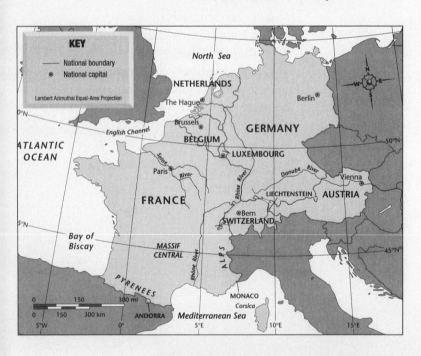

France is one of the largest countries in Central Western Europe.

■ REVIEW QUESTIONS

1. Where is the center of France's manufacturing region?

2. Map Skills What countries of Central Western Europe border France?

TEXT SUMMARY

The area that is now Germany was divided for hundreds of years into small states. Prussia began to unite the German states in the late 1700s. Germany was defeated in World War I and had to pay the winning countries **reparations**, money for war damages. The payments caused economic hardships and **inflation**, quickly rising prices. In 1929, many Germans lost their jobs during a worldwide economic depression.

In the early 1930s, Adolf Hitler and his Nazi party took power. Hitler blamed Jews and others for Germany's problems. In 1939, Germany invaded Poland, beginning World War II. The Nazis killed millions of Jews and other people in concentration camps. Germany was finally defeated in 1945.

After World War II, Germany was divided into Communist East Germany and democratic West Germany. In November 1989, the Berlin Wall, which had divided East and West Berlin, came down. The two countries reunited in October 1990.

Germany has three geographic regions. The south has high mountains, the center has hills, low peaks, and plateaus, and the north is flat.

Farming, manufacturing, and trade are important industries. The Rhine and Elbe rivers flow through one of the world's most important industrial centers. The Ruhr Valley, rich in coal, produces most of Germany's iron and steel. Germany rebuilt its economy after World War II. By 1999, it was the leading industrial country in Western Europe.

THE **BIG** IDEA

Germany is Europe's leading industrial nation. It was united again in 1990 after having been two separate countries since the end of World War II.

GRAPHIC SUMMARY:
Germany

Germany's coast is on the North Sea and the Baltic Sea.

REVIEW QUESTIONS

1. Why is the Ruhr Valley important to Germany?

2. Map Skills What mountain range is in southern Germany?

SECTION 3 THE BENELUX COUNTRIES

TEXT SUMMARY

THE BIG IDEA

Belgium, the Netherlands, and Luxembourg are the Benelux countries. They are all small and have low, flat land.

The word Benelux comes from the first letters of Belgium, Netherlands, and Luxembourg. They are also called the Low Countries because so much of their land is low and flat. They are small in area, but their total population is almost as large as Canada's.

One fifth of the Netherlands is land taken from the sea. When the Romans conquered the area, they built **dikes**, walls of earth and rock to hold back the sea. Later, the Dutch people reclaimed land by building dikes around a piece of land and pumping water out into canals. They call this reclaimed land a **polder**. Beginning in the 1200s, the Dutch used windmills to power the pumps that remove water from the land. The Dutch use more than half their land for agriculture.

Belgium has two main ethnic groups who speak different languages. The Walloons speak French. The Flemings speak Flemish, a dialect of Dutch. For many years, French was the only official language, even though more people spoke Flemish. In 1898, Flemish also became an official language. More recently, Belgium **decentralized** its government. It transferred power to smaller regions.

Luxembourg is the smallest Benelux country. Its people speak French, German, and Luxembourgish, a dialect of German. Luxembourg has one of the highest standards of living in Europe. It has many high-tech businesses and service industries. It trades mostly with other countries of the European Union.

GRAPHIC SUMMARY: *Countries of Central Western Europe*

Country	Population	Life Expectancy	Per Capita GDP (in US $)
Austria	8,133,611	77.3	25,550
Belgium	10,174,922	77.3	23,800
France	58,804,944	78.5	23,760
Germany	82,079,454	77	25,490
Liechtenstein	31,717	78	NA
Luxembourg	425,017	77.5	40,840
Netherlands	15,731,112	78	23,080
Switzerland	7,260,357	78.9	36,010

Source: Microsoft Encarta Interactive World Atlas 2000 NA indicates data not available

Luxembourg has the second highest GDP in Central Western Europe.

REVIEW QUESTIONS

1. How do the Dutch use the land they took from the sea?
2. **Chart Skills** Which Benelux country has the largest population?

SWITZERLAND AND AUSTRIA

■ TEXT SUMMARY

The Alps cover more than half the area of both Switzerland and Austria. Both countries are landlocked, meaning they do not have a coast on the sea.

Switzerland has three official languages: French, German, and Italian. The country is a confederation, a loose organization of states. It was formed in 1291 when three **cantons**, or states, united. Today, there are 26 cantons in the confederation. Each has its own language, religion, customs, and ways of making a living. Switzerland is **neutral**, and has not taken sides in wars between other countries in more than 200 years.

The Swiss have one of the world's highest standards of living. Milk from dairy farms is used in making chocolate and cheese. Switzerland is also known for products like watches, which need skilled labor.

Austria has had its present borders only since the end of World War I. For many years before then, it was part of the Austro-Hungarian Empire. The empire controlled much of Eastern Europe in the late 1800s.

It collapsed after its defeat in World War I.

Austrians speak German. Most people live in the eastern lowlands, where land is flat or hilly. Austria has mineral resources, such as iron ore, which are used for industry. Other economic activities include dairy farming and manufacturing. Vienna, the capital, was once one of the world's largest cities.

THE BIG IDEA

The people of Switzerland have very different cultural traditions from one another. Austria has been independent for a short time.

Austria and Switzerland's strong economies have enabled them to take in many refugees.

■ GRAPHIC SUMMARY:
Refugees to Western Europe

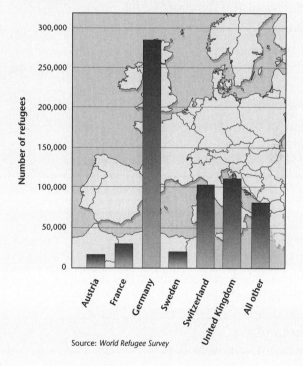

Source: *World Refugee Survey*

■ REVIEW QUESTIONS

1. Which war brought an end to the Austro-Hungarian Empire?

2. **Graph Skills** About how many refugees have gone to Switzerland?

CHAPTER 16 *Test*

◼ IDENTIFYING MAIN IDEAS

Write the letter of the correct answer in the blank provided. (10 points each)

____ **1.** What region of France is the main manu-facturing center?
   A. the Paris Basin
   B. the southwest
   C. the Rhône Valley
   D. the area around Bordeaux

____ **2.** A tunnel through the Alps connects France and
   A. Germany.
   B. the Netherlands.
   C. Austria.
   D. Italy.

____ **3.** The river that forms part of the border between France and Germany is the
   A. Rhône.
   B. Rhine.
   C. Ruhr.
   D. Elbe.

____ **4.** What are reparations?
   A. a time of rising prices
   B. money to pay for war damages
   C. the work of bringing private companies under government control
   D. repairs of government buildings

____ **5.** What happened to Germany immediately after World War II?
   A. It was reunited as one country.
   B. Many people lost their jobs after a worldwide depression.
   C. It was divided into East Germany and West Germany.
   D. The Berlin Wall came down.

____ **6.** What is the leading industrial country in Western Europe?
   A. France
   B. Germany
   C. Switzerland
   D. Luxembourg

____ **7.** What is a polder?
   A. land that was lost to the ocean
   B. land that was reclaimed from the sea
   C. walls of earth to hold back the sea
   D. a canal in the Netherlands

____ **8.** What are the two languages of Belgium?
   A. French and German
   B. German and Dutch
   C. Dutch and Flemish
   D. Flemish and French

____ **9.** What is a confederation?
   A. a loose group of states
   B. states united with a strong central government
   C. a country that has no states
   D. a country ruled by a stronger country

____ **10.** How long has Austria had its present borders?
   A. since it was the Austro-Hungarian Empire
   B. since the 1800s
   C. since the end of World War I
   D. since the end of World War II

Mediterranean Europe

SECTION 1 SPAIN AND PORTUGAL

◼ TEXT SUMMARY

Two countries—Spain and Portugal—dominate the Iberian Peninsula. The Pyrenees Mountains separate the peninsula from the rest of Europe. Reaching Spain by water is also difficult because steep cliffs rise along the coast.

The *Meseta*, or plateau, covers central Spain. Several rivers cross the Meseta, but only the Guadalquivir is **navigable**, deep and wide enough for ships.

Spain has a Mediterranean climate with mild, rainy winters and hot, dry summers. Little rain, however, reaches the Meseta, which is dry. Farmers there grow wheat and barley. **Siroccos**—hot, dry winds from northern Africa—make the southeast even drier.

Spain is developing new industries, such as transportation equipment. Bilbao and Barcelona are centers of industry. Madrid is the capital and largest city.

Many people in Spain identify with their regions. The Basques of northern Spain speak a language that is not related to any other European language. Some Basques want independence from Spain. People in other regions want more local control.

Portugal gets good rainfall for farming. Wheat, corn, and barley grow well. The country exports olive oil and cork.

Portugal became a trading nation in the 1100s. By the 1400s, Portuguese explorers had found routes around Africa to East Asia. Both Spain and Portugal had colonies in Latin America. Portugal also had colonies in Africa. They started to lose their colonies in the 1800s.

THE **BIG** IDEA

Spain and Portugal share the Iberian Peninsula. Mountains separate the peninsula from the rest of Europe.

◼ GRAPHIC SUMMARY:
Iberian Peninsula

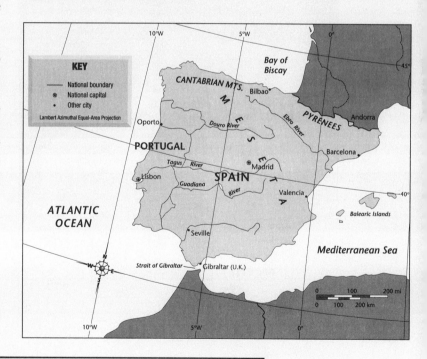

The countries of Spain and Portugal are located on the Iberian Peninsula.

◼ REVIEW QUESTIONS

1. On what peninsula are Spain and Portugal located?

2. Map Skills On what body of water is Lisbon located?

SECTION 2 · ITALY

■ TEXT SUMMARY

THE BIG IDEA

Italy is mountain-
ous, but agriculture
is important to the
economy. Many Ital-
ians have moved to
the industrial
north to find jobs.

Many people recognize Italy's boot shape on a map. The Apennine Mountains run all the way down the Italian Peninsula. The Alps form the northern border.

Until the 1960s, more than one third of the population lived and worked on farms. Today only 10 percent of the people are farmers. Italian factories make automobiles, home appliances, and other metal goods. The European Union has given Italy a larger market for its goods.

After the Roman Empire collapsed, many Italian cities became independent states. As Christianity spread, the Roman Catholic Church gained control of large amounts of land.

In 1861, states in the north joined to form the country of Italy. Within ten years, the peninsula was united. There are still great differences among Italy's regions.

The heart of the northern region is the Po River valley. This is Italy's best farmland. About two thirds of Italy's factory goods are made there.

Central Italy includes Rome, the capital. Inside Rome is Vatican City, the center of the Roman Catholic Church. Cities in central Italy became famous during the **Renaissance**, a time of great art and learning that started in Italy in the 1300s.

Southern Italy includes the islands of Sicily and Sardinia. The poor soil makes farming hard. Many people have moved to the north to find jobs.

■ GRAPHIC SUMMARY:
Italy

Italy is almost completely surrounded by water.

■ REVIEW QUESTIONS

1. Why have many southern Italians moved to the north?

2. **Map Skills** What mountains form Italy's northern border?

TEXT SUMMARY

History and geography make Greece part of the Mediterranean region. The culture that began in Greece developed further in Western Europe. Greece also has ties to Eastern Europe and Turkey, which it borders.

Greece includes some 2,000 islands. Most of the country is covered by mountains and rocky soil. Farmers raise sheep and goats on the slopes. Wheat, olives, and citrus fruits are grown on the narrow coastal plains.

Athens, the capital, is a modern city with ancient monuments. Over one third of all Greeks live in and near Athens.

Greece depends on the sea for trade. It has one of the world's largest fleets of ships as well as a shipbuilding industry. Fishing and tourism are also important.

The sea also keeps Greece connected to its islands. Fewer than two hundred of the islands are **inhabitable**, or able to support a permanent population. The island of Crete puzzles people. About thirty-five hundred years ago, it was a center of culture and trade. Around 1500 B.C., the culture declined. Nobody today can fully explain why.

Western culture has many of its roots in ancient Greece. From the second century B.C. to the fifth century A.D., Greece was part of the Roman Empire. Then it became part of the Byzantine Empire. The Turks ruled Greece for nearly 400 years until Greece gained its independence in 1829.

> ### THE **BIG** IDEA
>
> **Greece is mountainous and has an agricultural economy. It has relied on the sea for trade throughout its history.**

GRAPHIC SUMMARY: *Comparing Four Mediterranean Countries*

Country	Population	Life Expectancy	Per Capita GDP (in US $)
Greece	10,662,138	78.3	11,740
Italy	56,782,748	78.4	19,910
Portugal	9,927,556	75.7	10,270
Spain	39,133,996	77.6	13,530

Source: *Microsoft Encarta Interactive World Atlas 2000*

Greece and Portugal are similar in size of population and per capita GDP.

REVIEW QUESTIONS

1. What makes Greece a part of the Mediterranean region?

2. **Chart Skills** Which country has the highest population? Which one has the lowest life expectancy?

CHAPTER 17 *Test*

◨ IDENTIFYING MAIN IDEAS

Write the letter of the correct answer in the blank provided. (10 points each)

_____ 1. What mountains separate the Iberian Peninsula from the rest of Europe?
  A. the Pyrenees
  B. the Alps
  C. the Apennines
  D. the Meseta

_____ 2. What is a sirocco?
  A. a form of money used in Spain
  B. the kind of climate found in Iberia
  C. a warm current of water
  D. a hot wind from northern Africa

_____ 3. How are the Basques different from other people in Spain?
  A. They speak a language that is not related to other languages of Europe.
  B. They speak only Spanish.
  C. They want stronger ties with the Spanish government.
  D. They have better farmland than other people in Spain.

_____ 4. Where did Portugal once have colonies?
  A. in North America and Antarctica
  B. in North America and South America
  C. in Africa and Latin America
  D. in northern Asia

_____ 5. Where are most of Italy's factories located?
  A. in the south of the country
  B. in the center of the country
  C. in the north of the country
  D. in Sardinia and Sicily

_____ 6. Where is Italy's best farmland?
  A. in the north, in the Po River valley
  B. in the southern islands of Sardinia and Sicily
  C. in the southern tip of Italy's boot
  D. in the central part of the country

_____ 7. What was the Renaissance?
  A. the period when Italy was united as one country
  B. a time of great art and learning
  C. a time when people had to move to find work
  D. the age when most factories were opened

_____ 8. Which has Greece always depended on for trade?
  A. airports
  B. the European Union
  C. the sea
  D. highways

_____ 9. Which place would be considered *uninhabitable*?
  A. a place with a large permanent population
  B. a place that cannot support a permanent population
  C. a place with a small permanent population
  D. a place with many tourists

_____ 10. What industry is important in Greece?
  A. manufacturing automobiles
  B. road-building
  C. airplane construction
  D. shipbuilding

Regional Atlas

INTRODUCTION TO CENTRAL EUROPE AND NORTHERN EURASIA

■ TEXT SUMMARY

Central Europe and Northern Eurasia spans two continents in the Northern Hemisphere. The land is generally flat in the west and rises higher in the east and the south. The region is covered in broad plains, which allowed for movement throughout history.

The climates of the region range from Mediterranean to subarctic. Irkutsk, Russia, has the coldest winters of any place in the world besides Antarctica.

The **tundra**, a treeless plain in arctic areas where short grasses and mosses grow, covers northern Russia. Coniferous forests, called **taiga**, and grasslands, called the **steppe**, are found across Central Europe and in Russia.

A history of migration has resulted in a **multiethnic** region, containing many ethnic groups. Although **communism**, a system in which the government controlled almost all aspects of political and economic life, restricted religion, Orthodox Christianity is an important faith in Central Europe.

In the 1980s, the fall of communism resulted in a move to capitalism. Industrial activities have led to pollution and acid rain. The fall of communism affected the level of health care in many nations.

THE BIG IDEA

Central Europe and Northern Eurasia covers a vast area. There are great physical, climatic, cultural, and economic differences between the western and eastern portions of this region.

■ GRAPHIC SUMMARY: *Central Europe and Northern Eurasia*

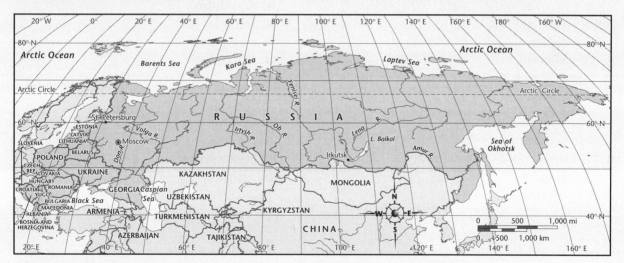

The borders of the countries of Central Europe and Northern Eurasia have changed often.

■ REVIEW QUESTIONS

1. How has the geography of Central Europe and Northern Eurasia affected the movement of people across the region?

2. Map Skills What country of Central Europe and Northern Eurasia is the largest?

CHAPTER 18 *Test*

■ IDENTIFYING MAIN IDEAS

Write the letter of the correct answer in the blank provided. (10 points each)

____ 1. Central Europe and Northern Eurasia spans
   A. four countries.
   B. one continent.
   C. two continents.
   D. three countries.

____ 2. What common geographical feature of Central Europe and Northern Eurasia has allowed for easy migration?
   A. low mountains
   B. broad plains
   C. high mountains
   D. coniferous forests

____ 3. In which hemisphere does Central Europe and Northern Eurasia lie?
   A. Western Hemisphere
   B. Eastern Hemisphere
   C. Southern Hemisphere
   D. Northern Hemisphere

____ 4. What city is the coldest place in the world, besides Antarctica?
   A. Irkutsk, Russia
   B. Minsk, Belarus
   C. Prague, Czech Republic
   D. Warsaw, Poland

____ 5. Taiga is
   A. deciduous forest.
   B. coniferous forest.
   C. grassland.
   D. desert scrub.

____ 6. The steppe ecosystem
   A. is a fertile region used for farming.
   B. is a mountainous region used for herding animals.
   C. is a frigid region with little wildlife.
   D. is found only in Russia.

____ 7. The tundra ecosystem can be found in
   A. Yugoslavia.
   B. Romania.
   C. Russia.
   D. Albania.

____ 8. A region that is multiethnic has
   A. many forests.
   B. many ethnic groups.
   C. an official language.
   D. no official language.

____ 9. What religion is important in many Central European countries?
   A. Buddhism
   B. Islam
   C. Christianity
   D. Hinduism

____ 10. Before the 1980s, the national economies of the region were
   A. Marxist.
   B. capitalist.
   C. communist.
   D. democratic.

Central and Eastern Europe

 **SECTION 1** *POLAND*

■ TEXT SUMMARY

Poland has been conquered many times. Yet the Polish people have kept their **national identity**, or sense of what makes them a nation. Their attachment to the land has helped them keep their national identity. So has their religion. Ninety-five percent of the people are Roman Catholic.

Poland was a multiethnic country before World War II. Three million Jews lived in Poland. During the war, the Nazis forced Jews to live in **ghettoes**, city areas where minorities must live. Later the Nazis built six major concentration camps, or prison camps, in Poland. People from many countries, especially Jews, were murdered in these camps. By the end of the war, about 6 million Poles had been killed in concentration camps. Half of them were Jews. In all, the Nazis murdered more than 6 million European Jews. This destruction of human life is called the **Holocaust**.

After the war, a Communist government supported by the Soviet Union controlled Poland. It tried to do away with religion, but the Roman Catholic Church remained strong.

During the 1980s, a Polish labor union called Solidarity began to demand economic reforms and more freedom. Poland finally held free elections in 1989.

After communism ended, it was hard to turn state-controlled businesses into private businesses. Prices rose quickly. Many people lost their jobs. By the mid-1990s, the economy started to improve.

> ### THE **BIG** IDEA
>
> The Polish people kept their culture even when others ruled their country. A love of their land and belief in their religion helped shape the Polish identity.

■ GRAPHIC SUMMARY:
Poland

Poland's coast on the Baltic Sea provides a good opportunity for trade.

■ REVIEW QUESTIONS

1. What helped Poles keep their national identity?

2. Map Skills Why do you think Gdańsk is an important city?

THE CZECH AND SLOVAK REPUBLICS, AND HUNGARY

■ TEXT SUMMARY

THE BIG IDEA

The three countries have shifted to free-market economies. Hungary's economy is improving, the Czech Republic has done well, but Slovakia has been struggling.

The Czechs, Slovaks, and Hungarians share historical links with Western Europe. But their countries have major differences.

After World War I, Czechoslovakia became a new nation with two main groups—Czechs and Slovaks. After World War II, the Soviet Union placed a Communist government in Czechoslovakia. In the late 1980s, Czechoslovakia ended Communist rule. In 1993, it divided peacefully into the Czech Republic and Slovak Republic—also called Slovakia.

■ GRAPHIC SUMMARY:
The Czech Republic, Slovakia, and Hungary

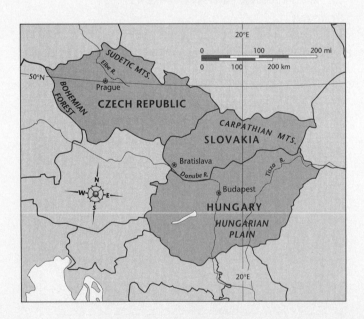

None of these three countries has a seacoast.

The Czech Republic began **privatization**, or selling government businesses to private companies. The country has many industries, but many factories are old, and pollution is a serious problem.

Slovakia has a mixed economy of manufacturing and farming. The Communists turned private farms into **collective farms**, where farmers were paid by the government and shared profits. Slovakia is now trying to return farms to private owners. Slovakia has political problems as well as a struggling economy.

About 90 percent of Hungarians are Magyars. Hungary became a nation in the year 1000. It fought off many foreign rulers but could not drive out the Soviet-backed Communist government. In 1990, Hungarians elected their first democratic government in over forty years. It began to return businesses to private companies.

The fertile farm region east of the Danube River in Hungary is called "the breadbasket of Europe."

■ REVIEW QUESTIONS

1. What united these countries in the years after World War II?

2. **Map Skills** What river forms part of the border between Slovakia and Hungary?

THE BALKAN PENINSULA

TEXT SUMMARY

The Balkan Peninsula was ruled by the Turks for 500 years. After World War I, the region broke up into small unfriendly countries. This event led to a new word—**balkanize**. Communists controlled the Balkans after 1948. In the late 1980s, these countries began to overthrow their Communist governments.

Under communism, Romania had serious economic problems. Several leaders promised reform, but the economy grew worse. A United States soft drink maker has helped **entrepreneurs** start shops to sell soft drinks. Entrepreneurs are people who start and build businesses.

Bulgaria has fertile soil and mild weather. It is known as the garden of Eastern Europe. Bulgaria has a democratic government, but Communists still play a large role. By the mid-1990s, Bulgaria had found foreign markets for its goods and was welcoming tourists to its Black Sea resorts.

Albania's Communist leaders kept the country isolated. It became one of the poorest countries in Europe. Since it became democractic in the early 1990s, companies from other countries have opened factories in Albania because wages are low.

After World War I, Yugoslavia became a new country with many ethnic groups that did not get along. After Communist control ended, four of its republics declared independence. Only Serbia and Montenegro stayed in Yugoslavia. Fighting began between the newly independent countries and among their ethnic groups. The worst fighting was in Bosnia-Herzegovina.

> ## THE **BIG** IDEA
>
> The countries of the Balkan Peninsula share a history of conflict and foreign control. Many countries are multiethnic.

GRAPHIC SUMMARY: *The Breakup of Yugoslavia*

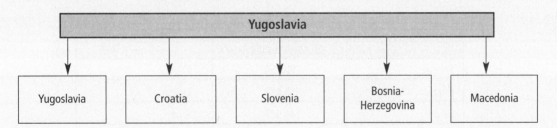

Many countries in the Balkan Peninsula are small, but Yugoslavia broke up into even smaller countries.

REVIEW QUESTIONS

1. What does the word balkanize mean?

2. **Chart Skills** How many countries were created when Yugoslavia broke up?

Guide to the Essentials **CHAPTER 19**

BALTIC STATES AND BORDER NATIONS

■ TEXT SUMMARY

The Baltic states and border nations along Russia's western edge were once republics within the Soviet Union. After 1991, these republics became independent nations.

Lithuania, Latvia, and Estonia are mainly flat with fertile plains. The Baltic Sea has brought both trade and invasion. Soviet forces invaded in 1939 and **annexed**, or formally added, the Baltic states to the Soviet Union.

Since independence, the Baltic states have privatized industries and encouraged foreign investment and trade. They have also begun to **diversify**, or increase the variety of, their industries.

Ukraine was where the first Russian state began over 1,000 years ago. Under Communist Soviet rule, Ukrainians were forced to work on collective farms. Ukrainians protested by burning crops. In response, Soviet forces seized all grain. As a result, 5 to 8 million Ukrainians starved to death. In 1986, an explosion destroyed a nuclear reactor in Chernobyl, causing severe damage to human life and the environment.

Ukraine has large fertile plains and huge coal resources. The export of its many farm products has helped the economy. But outdated machinery, lack of foreign investment, and the need to import oil hold Ukraine back from economic prosperity.

Unlike other former republics, Belarus favors its close ties with Russia. It has strong industrial and service industries, as well as oil, but it must import most of the resources needed for its industries.

Moldova is the most densely populated of the former republics. It was once ruled by Romania, and Romanian is now the language used in schools.

THE **BIG** IDEA

The nations of this region were once republics within the Soviet Union. Since independence in 1991, they have struggled to improve their economies.

■ GRAPHIC SUMMARY: *Baltic States and Border Nations*

COUNTRY	AREA (in square miles)	CAPITAL
Belarus	80,154	Minsk
Estonia	17,413	Tallinn
Latvia	24,942	Riga
Lithuania	25,174	Vilnius
Moldova	13,012	Chisinau
Ukraine	233,089	Kiev

Source: *Microsoft Encarta Interactive World Atlas 2000*

All of these nations were once part of the Soviet Union.

■ REVIEW QUESTIONS

1. What have the Baltic states done since independence to improve their economies?

2. **Chart Skills** What is the largest nation in the Baltic states and border nations region? What is the smallest?

CHAPTER 19 *Test*

◼ IDENTIFYING MAIN IDEAS

Write the letter of the correct answer in the blank provided. (10 points each)

____ **1.** What is a ghetto?
   A. an agricultural area
   B. an industrial region
   C. an area where a minority group has to live
   D. an area where people go to build farms

____ **2.** The murder of Jews, Poles, and other people by the Nazis during World War II is called
   A. a ghetto.
   B. a concentration camp.
   C. the Holocaust.
   D. Communist.

____ **3.** In Poland, Solidarity is
   A. the name of the communist government.
   B. the Soviet government which ruled Poland.
   C. a labor union that fought for reform.
   D. the nickname of the president.

____ **4.** Czechoslovakia split into two countries
   A. in a war.
   B. after Communists ordered the split.
   C. because of privatization.
   D. peacefully.

____ **5.** When a country starts privatization, it
   A. sells government-owned businesses to private companies.
   B. sells private companies to the government.
   C. investigates people's private lives.
   D. takes property from private citizens.

____ **6.** Hungary is called "the breadbasket of Europe" because
   A. of its fertile farm region.
   B. it bakes more bread than any other country.
   C. its people eat more bread than those of any other country.
   D. of its special kind of breadbaskets.

____ **7.** What is an entrepreneur?
   A. a person who works on a government farm
   B. a person who works in a government-owned business
   C. a person who starts and builds a business
   D. a political leader

____ **8.** Why did Yugoslavia break up?
   A. It had no central government.
   B. Its people could not earn a living.
   C. Most people wanted to return to communism.
   D. The different ethnic groups did not get along.

____ **9.** When the Baltic states were annexed by the Soviet Union they were
   A. cut off from Soviet support.
   B. formally added to the Soviet Union.
   C. targets for Soviet missiles.
   D. freed from Soviet control.

____ **10.** The Chernobyl nuclear explosion occurred in
   A. Belarus.
   B. Romania.
   C. Ukraine.
   D. Estonia.

Russia

SECTION 1 REGIONS OF RUSSIA

▪ TEXT SUMMARY

Russia is the world's largest country. It stretches across ten time zones, encompassing a varied terrain. The land is fairly flat, consisting mainly of plateaus and rolling plains.

The Ural Mountains divide Europe from Asia. These low mountains contain great mineral wealth. Russia has many rivers, including the Ob, Yenisey, and Lena, which flow into the Arctic Ocean. The Volga River, Europe's longest river, drains into the Caspian Sea, the world's largest lake.

The ecosystems are closely related to location and climate. The climate is main-

ly continental or subarctic. Along the arctic shore is an area of **tundra**, a largely treeless region with only tiny plants and animal life that can survive the polar conditions. Forests cover almost half of Russia and are home to many animals, including the sable and the brown bear. The fertile soil of Russia's grasslands, called **chernozem**, provides nutrients for growing crops.

The Asian part of Russia is known as Siberia. A cool and swampy area, it has a layer of **permafrost**, or permanently frozen soil. It has rich reserves of minerals and oil, but its harsh climate and terrain making mining these resources very difficult.

> ### THE **BIG** IDEA
>
> Russia is the largest country on earth. It has rich natural resources, but its size and climate make it hard to develop them.

▪ GRAPHIC SUMMARY: *Russia*

Russia stretches across eastern Europe and northern Asia.

▪ REVIEW QUESTIONS

1. What is chernozem?

2. Map Skills What is the capital of Russia?

EMERGENCE OF RUSSIA

■ TEXT SUMMARY

Modern Russia began in the 800s, when Vikings established a state in what is now Kiev, Ukraine. The Slavic people who lived there accepted the state. Orthodox Christianity became the main religion of the region.

Mongol warriors conquered the area, but Russia regained control and set up a series of monarchs, called **czars**, to rule the land. Under the czars, the nation expanded its borders.

In 1812 Napoleon of France invaded Russia, capturing Moscow. The Russians burned their cities as they fled, and Napoleon began leading his troops back to France. However, the troops were unprepared for Russia's harsh climate and terrain. Almost all of Napoleon's men died on this return trip. By the twentieth century, Russia controlled nearly all of northern Eurasia.

The Russian Revolution in 1917 caused the czar to **abdicate**, or give up his crown. The revolutionaries established a Communist dictatorship called the Union of Soviet Socialist Republics, or the Soviet Union.

The Soviet Union had a **command economy**, which meant the government decided what goods would be produced. The government also controlled people's lives. Those who complained were sent to prison and labor camps or killed.

In the late 1980s, a new leader, Mikhail Gorbachev, introduced a policy of **glasnost**, or openness, that allowed people to speak freely. The government also offered a plan for **perestroika**, or economic restructuring. This called for a gradual change from a command economy to private ownership.

Since the end of 1991, Russia's government has become democratic, but Communist beliefs are still held by a large number of the population.

THE **BIG** IDEA

Russia's history is one of conquest and invasion. The command economy of the Soviet Union led to poverty and dissatisfaction with the government. Since the 1990s, Russia has made many efforts to improve its economy and standard of living.

■ GRAPHIC SUMMARY: *Events in Russia up to the Russian Revolution*

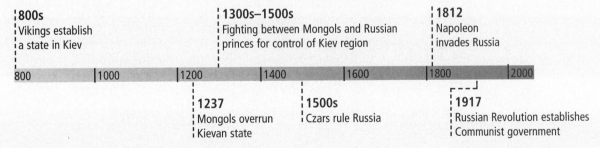

800s
Vikings establish a state in Kiev

1300s–1500s
Fighting between Mongols and Russian princes for control of Kiev region

1812
Napoleon invades Russia

800 | 1000 | 1200 | 1400 | 1600 | 1800 | 2000

1237
Mongols overrun Kievan state

1500s
Czars rule Russia

1917
Russian Revolution establishes Communist government

Russia has experienced many invasions and conquests.

■ REVIEW QUESTIONS

1. What policies did the Russian government establish during the late 1980s?

2. **Time Line Skills** What happened in 1237 in Russia?

SECTION 3 GEOGRAPHIC ISSUES IN RUSSIA

■ TEXT SUMMARY

More than 80 percent of Russia's inhabitants consider themselves Russian, the descendants of the Slavic peoples. Almost three fourths of Russia's people live in urban areas. However, traditional ways of life continue in villages and rural areas.

About 25 million residents of Russia belong to non-Russian ethnic groups. Intense ethnic conflict has occurred in the republics within the Caucasus region. The worst fighting has taken place in Chechnya. Desiring independence, Chechens fought a guerrilla war against Russian control during the 1990s. After a three-year cease-fire, fighting between the two countries resumed.

Transportation within Russia has been a challenge. Travel by road is slow and almost impossible during winter months. Air travel is costly and unsuitable for the transport of resources. The many rivers in Russia provide a good method of transport, but they too cannot be used in the winter when they are frozen. Railroads are the most important means of transportation. Several major railroad systems run through the nation, including the great Trans-Siberian Railroad.

Changing from a command economy to a market economy has been difficult for Russia. Consumer goods are scarce and unemployment is high. Financial instability led to the growth of a **black market**, through which goods and services move unofficially without formal record keeping.

Russia faces many other challenges. The health of the population has declined since the 1990s. Intense industrialization depleted natural resources and contaminated many urban areas and bodies of water. Lack of money hinders Russia's ability to solve these problems.

> **THE BIG IDEA**
>
> **Russia faces many challenges. Ethnic conflict, insufficient transportation, and pollution have left many in the nation struggling.**

■ GRAPHIC SUMMARY: *Comparing Russia and the United States*

Country	Population	Life Expectancy (years)	Per Capita GDP (in U.S. $)
Russia	146,861,022	65	3,030
United States	270,311,758	76.1	33,900

Sources: *Microsoft Encarta Interactive World Atlas 2000* and *CIA World Factbook 2000*

Russia's demographic data differs greatly from that of the United States.

■ REVIEW QUESTIONS

1. How many people living in Russia consider themselves Russian?

2. **Chart Skills** Which nation has a stronger economy—Russia or the United States? Why?

CHAPTER 20 *Test*

■ IDENTIFYING MAIN IDEAS

Write the letter of the correct answer in the blank provided. (10 points each)

____ **1.** Europe's longest river is the
  A. Volga.
  B. Lena.
  C. Ob.
  D. Yenisey.

____ **2.** The climate of Russia is mainly
  A. continental and Mediterranean.
  B. subarctic and continental.
  C. arid and subarctic.
  D. semiarid and continental.

____ **3.** What is chernozem?
  A. Russia's national flower
  B. a type of spice found in Siberia
  C. a small town in northern Russia
  D. the fertile soil of Russia's grasslands

____ **4.** Permafrost can be found
  A. in Siberia.
  B. in the Caucasus Mountains.
  C. around the Caspian Sea.
  D. along the Ob River.

____ **5.** Where was the first Russian state established?
  A. Kiev, Ukraine
  B. Bucharest, Romania
  C. Minsk, Belarus
  D. Moscow, Russia

____ **6.** What is a czar?
  A. a communist leader
  B. a Russian monarch
  C. a Siberian king
  D. a modern president

____ **7.** What is the name of the Communist dictatorship that ruled much of Northern Eurasia?
  A. the Russia Empire
  B. the Ural Republic
  C. Siberia
  D. the Soviet Union

____ **8.** Perestroika is
  A. a plan for economic restructuring.
  B. a policy of openness.
  C. the type of economy adopted by the Soviet Union.
  D. a type of Russian dance.

____ **9.** The most important method of transportation in Russia is the
  A. airplane.
  B. boat.
  C. train.
  D. car.

____ **10.** Russia
  A. lacks industrialization.
  B. has a command economy.
  C. has little unemployment.
  D. has severe pollution problems.

Regional Atlas

INTRODUCTION TO CENTRAL AND SOUTHWEST ASIA

◼ TEXT SUMMARY

THE **BIG** IDEA

For hundreds of years, cultures have exchanged goods and ideas and often clashed in this region. Judaism, Christianity, and Islam developed there.

The Fertile Crescent in Southwest Asia was the birthplace of civilization and agriculture. Around 8000 B.C., people began to plant crops and raise livestock in a process called the **agricultural revolution**.

Central and Southwest Asia's location made it a target for invasion. After World War I, European powers divided the region. Once all countries gained independence, conflict remained as nations fought for land control.

The region, covered mainly with mountains and plains, is mostly arid or semiarid. Seaside areas have steady temperatures, while inland areas have cold winters and hot summers.

Most of the region has a desert ecosystem. The **chaparral** ecosystem, with drought-resistant herbs and bushes, is found near the Black and Mediterranean seas. Pollution and **poaching**, or illegal hunting, threaten the wildlife of the Caspian Sea.

Three major religions began in the region: Judaism, Christianity, and Islam. All are based on **monotheism**, a belief in one God. Most people in the region are Muslims. Religious differences have led to many conflicts. Such conflict is severe in Jerusalem, a sacred city to all three religions.

Most of the population lives in urban areas, where the main economic activities are services and industry. The region contains large reserves of oil and natural gas.

Water shortages are a challenge for the region. Some nations have built **desalination plants**, where seawater is evaporated to obtain fresh water.

The countries in this region rely on trade. Most countries in this region export large amounts of oil to get the goods and foods they need.

◼ GRAPHIC SUMMARY:
Central and Southwest Asia

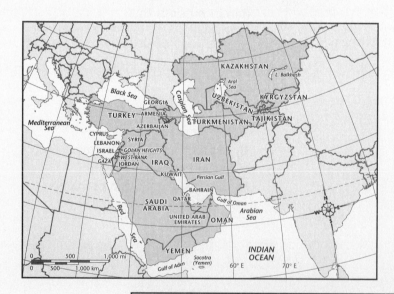

Central and Southwest Asia is a region surrounded by three continents.

◼ REVIEW QUESTIONS

1. What three monotheistic religions began in Southwest Asia?

2. Map Skills Which four Central and Southwest Asian countries border the Caspian Sea?

CHAPTER 21 *Test*

■ IDENTIFYING MAIN IDEAS

Write the letter of the correct answer in the blank provided. (10 points each)

____ **1.** The agricultural revolution can be described as
   A. a great migration from urban to rural areas.
   B. replacing old ways of farming with modern machinery.
   C. the time when people began planting crops and raising livestock.
   D. the trade of crops with foreign nations.

____ **2.** The climate of the region is mostly
   A. Mediterranean and subtropical.
   B. arid and semiarid.
   C. semiarid and subtropical.
   D. arid and subarctic.

____ **3.** Where are steady temperatures most likely to be found?
   A. seaside
   B. inland
   C. in Tajikistan
   D. central Iran

____ **4.** What is chaparral?
   A. a type of coniferous forest
   B. an area of drought-resistant bushes
   C. another name for a desert
   D. a wet, marshy area

____ **5.** In which body of water has poaching become a threat to the wildlife?
   A. Black Sea
   B. Mediterranean Sea
   C. Caspian Sea
   D. Red Sea

____ **6.** Monotheism is
   A. a belief in several gods.
   B. a belief in one god.
   C. a belief that God does not exist.
   D. a combination of several religions.

____ **7.** Most people in Central and Southwest Asia are
   A. Christian.
   B. Jewish.
   C. Buddhist.
   D. Muslim.

____ **8.** Where does most of the region's population live?
   A. in urban areas
   B. in rural areas
   C. in central Saudi Arabia
   D. near the Aral Sea

____ **9.** The region contains large reserves of what natural resource?
   A. coal
   B. gold
   C. phosphates
   D. oil

____ **10.** Desalination plants are used to
   A. pump oil out of the ground.
   B. convert saltwater to fresh water.
   C. clean urban areas.
   D. produce consumer goods.

The Caucasus and Central Asia

SECTION 1 *THE CAUCASUS NATIONS*

TEXT SUMMARY

The former Soviet republics of Georgia, Armenia, and Azerbaijan lie in the Caucasus Mountains. Many ethnic groups live here, and their differences have often led to violence.

Georgia is mountainous, with fertile river valleys. Tourists are attracted to the subtropical climate near the Black Sea. A continental climate is found inland.

After the fall of communism, the economy declined. Agriculture and machine manufacturing helped improve the economy after the mid-1990s. Georgia has increased the extraction of its manganese, coal, and oil reserves.

About 70 percent of Georgia's population are descendants of ethnic Georgians. Ethnic groups in the northern region seek **autonomy**, or independence, from Georgia.

Armenia is landlocked and has a rocky terrain. Farmers grow crops in southern valleys. Rug making is a traditional craft. The people are primarily Christian.

Armenia has had bitter relations with its neighbor Turkey. During World War I, Turks attempted to deport the people of Armenia. One third of all Armenians died en route or were killed in this act of **genocide**, the systematic killing or intentional destruction of a people.

Armenia has more recently fought with the Azeri people of Azerbaijan, a mainly Islamic nation. Both Azeris and Armenians have feelings of **nationalism**, the desire of a cultural group to rule themselves as a separate nation. This has led to violent conflicts.

Azerbaijan is on the western coast of the Caspian Sea. Rich deposits of oil are the nation's main source of wealth. Half the population are rural herders. Ninety percent of the population are ethnic Azeris. Most other ethnic groups fled as tensions intensified.

Azerbaijan's conflict with Armenia has caused severe economic problems. With no access to the Mediterranean and Black seas, Azerbaijan has trouble reaching world markets. Oil and chemical industries have caused great environmental damage.

> ### THE **BIG** IDEA
>
> After gaining independence in 1991, the Caucasus nations have had to cope with many ethnic and political issues. The nations of the region are still working to resolve conflict.

GRAPHIC SUMMARY:
The Caucasus Nations

Country	Land Area (sq. mi.)	Population	Projected Population 2025
Armenia	11,506	3,421,775	3,433,747
Azerbaijan	33,436	7,855,576	9,429,191
Georgia	26,911	5,108,527	4,718,035

The Caucasus nations may be small in size, but the diversity of their populations is large.

Sources: *Microsoft Encarta World Almanac 2000* and Population Reference Bureau

REVIEW QUESTIONS

1. What is genocide?

2. Chart Skills Which nation's population will decrease by 2025?

THE CENTRAL ASIAN NATIONS

SECTION 2

TEXT SUMMARY

Stretching from the Caspian Sea to mountain ranges along China's western border are the Central Asian nations of Kazakhstan, Kyrgyzstan, Tajikistan, Turkmenistan, and Uzbekistan.

Mountains are found in the southeast. In the east are two of Asia's largest deserts, the Kara Kum and the Kyzyl Kum. Central Asia's climate is mostly arid or semiarid.

Northern Kazakhstan has steppes and grassland with a rich topsoil called **chernozem**. This soil makes the region good for farming. Parts of Central Asia also have large reserves of oil and natural gas.

The Central Asian nations have diverse ethnic, religious, and language groups. Most people in the region are Islamic. Since independence, some leaders have supported Islamic fundamentalism. **Fundamentalism** is a set of religious beliefs based on a strict reading of a sacred text.

Traditionally, most Central Asians were nomadic herders. Under Soviet rule, people were forced to work on government farms. Industrialization was encouraged, spurring the growth of cities. Since independence, industry has grown and tourism has become important.

Rapid industrialization has led to environmental problems. Soviets diverted Central Asian rivers from the Aral Sea for irrigation. The amount of water reaching the Aral Sea decreased, causing the sea to shrink and become more salty. This has also lead to **desertification**, the extension of the desert landscape due to environmental changes caused by humans.

THE BIG IDEA

Kazakhstan, Kyrgyzstan, Tajikistan, Turkmenistan, and Uzbekistan make up Central Asia. Under Soviet rule, the people of these nations withstood dramatic changes to their cultures. Since independence, the nations of Central Asia have been developing their economies.

GRAPHIC SUMMARY: *Central Asia*

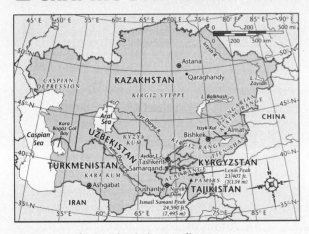

The terrain of Central Asia is very diverse.

REVIEW QUESTIONS

1. What is the most practiced religion in Central Asia?

2. Map Skills What Central Asian country is the largest?

CHAPTER 22 *Test*

◼ IDENTIFYING MAIN IDEAS

Write the letter of the correct answer in the blank provided. (10 points each)

_____ **1.** Between which two seas are the Caucasus nations?
  A. Aral and Black seas
  B. Caspian and Aral seas
  C. Mediterranean and Black seas
  D. Caspian and Black seas

_____ **2.** If a nation wants autonomy, what is it seeking?
  A. automatic dictatorship
  B. economic success
  C. independence
  D. free trade agreements

_____ **3.** Which country has trouble reaching world markets because of its location?
  A. Azerbaijan
  B. Armenia
  C. Georgia
  D. Russia

_____ **4.** Which nation lost one third of its population to genocide?
  A. Armenia
  B. Georgia
  C. Azerbaijan
  D. Turkey

_____ **5.** The desire of a cultural group to rule itself as a separate nation is called
  A. communism.
  B. fundamentalism.
  C. capitalism.
  D. nationalism.

_____ **6.** Minority ethnic groups have fled Azerbaijan
  A. in search of jobs.
  B. to find new land to farm.
  C. to escape religious and ethnic conflict.
  D. because the nation is overpopulated.

_____ **7.** Chernozem is rich soil found on the steppes of which nation?
  A. Kazakhstan
  B. Uzbekistan
  C. Turkmenistan
  D. Tajikistan

_____ **8.** Most people in Central Asia are
  A. Christian.
  B. Buddhist.
  C. Jewish.
  D. Muslim.

_____ **9.** When the Soviet Union controlled Central Asia
  A. people were forced to work on government farms.
  B. industrialization was discouraged.
  C. urban areas declined.
  D. most people became nomadic herders.

_____ **10.** What is desertification?
  A. the name for military troops who leave their posts unattended
  B. the irrigation of desert lands
  C. the lack of precipitation in an area that usually receives abundant rainfall
  D. the extension of the desert landscape due to environmental changes caused by humans

The Countries of Southwest Asia

 SECTION 1 ## CREATING THE MODERN MIDDLE EAST

■ TEXT SUMMARY

The Middle East, located on trade routes between Europe, Africa, and Asia, has been important for thousands of years. In the 600s, Muslims conquered the region. Most of the conquered people began to practice Islam and speak the Arabic language.

In the 900s, Seljuk Turks conquered most of the region. They became Muslims and ruled for more than 400 years. They lost control to the Ottoman Turks. By the late 1700s, the Ottoman Empire was weak and its many ethnic and religious groups wanted independence. The Ottoman Empire was defeated during World War I. The winning countries divided up the region.

Great Britain took Palestine as a **mandate,** or land governed for the League of Nations until it was ready for independence. Two groups—Arabs and Jews—claimed Palestine. In the late 1800s, many Jews had started moving to Palestine. Many were **Zionists** who wanted to make Palestine an independent Jewish country. Arabs in Palestine wanted **self-determination**, the right to decide their own future.

After World War II, the United Nations split Palestine into two states—one Jewish and one Arab. Jews accepted the plan, but Arabs did not. In 1948, Jews announced the independence of the new country of Israel. Hours later, neighboring Arab countries attacked. Israel won and controlled most of Palestine. Jordan and Egypt divided the rest. The Palestinians were left without a country.

> ### THE **BIG** IDEA
>
> After the Ottoman Empire fell at the end of World War I, it was divided into many countries. The 1948 war between Israel and the Arab countries left Palestinians without a homeland.

■ GRAPHIC SUMMARY: *Breakup of the Ottoman Empire*

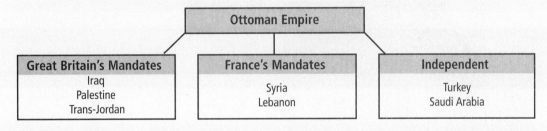

Ottoman Empire

Great Britain's Mandates	France's Mandates	Independent
Iraq	Syria	Turkey
Palestine	Lebanon	Saudi Arabia
Trans-Jordan		

Many new countries were created out of the Ottoman Empire.

■ REVIEW QUESTIONS

1. What two groups claimed Palestine?

2. Chart Skills What countries became British mandates?

SECTION 2 ISRAEL

■ TEXT SUMMARY

THE BIG IDEA

Israel has turned swamps and desert into good farmland and is a leader in technology. The country has a diverse population and is trying to achieve peace with its Arab neighbors.

When the first Zionists arrived in Palestine in the 1880s, they began to irrigate the desert and drain the swamps. Today the Negev Desert, which covers half of Israel, has been turned into fertile farmland. A process called **drip irrigation** is used to preserve water resources by letting precise amounts of water drip onto plants from pipes. Scientists made Israel a leader in high technology. The country also has many service industries. Minerals are mined from the Dead Sea, a huge saltwater lake.

About 80 percent of Israelis are Jewish. Before 1948, most came from Europe. Later, many Jews came from other countries in Southwest Asia and from North Africa. Many were poorer and less educated than European Jews. In recent years, many Jews have come from the former Soviet Union. Almost 20 percent of Israel's population is Arab.

During the 1948 war, many Palestinians lost their homes and fled to Arab countries. Even more Jews had to leave Arab countries. After another war in 1967, Israel took control of the West Bank in Jordan and the Gaza Strip. Many Palestinians fled from the West Bank and became refugees. Many of the refugee camps became bases for the Palestine Liberation Organization (PLO). It demanded that Palestine be freed and the refugees be allowed to return to their homes. The PLO refused to recognize Israel as a country. Some members were terrorists. Tensions remain high and violent outbreaks continue despite several peace agreements between Israel and the Palestinians.

■ GRAPHIC SUMMARY:
Israel and Its Neighbors

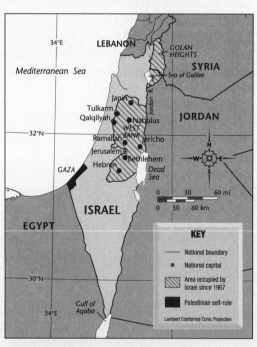

Israel is a small country surrounded by Arab neighbors.

■ REVIEW QUESTIONS

1. How has the land of Israel been changed?

2. **Map Skills** What four countries border Israel?

SECTION 3 JORDAN, LEBANON, SYRIA, AND IRAQ

◼ TEXT SUMMARY

The countries of Iraq, Jordan, Lebanon, and Syria are at the center of the problems that affect all of Southwest Asia.

Jordan lost its fertile farmland on the West Bank to Israel after the 1967 Arab-Israeli war. The affect on Jordan's economy was terrible. In addition, many Palestinian refugees fled to Jordan after the 1948 and 1967 wars. Many threatened to overthrow King Hussein if he did not support their struggle for a homeland.

For many years Lebanon had a strong economy. But civil wars among the country's Christian and Muslim groups left Lebanon in a state of **anarchy**, or lawlessness. Most of the fighting ended in the early 1990s, but peace is uncertain.

Throughout its history, Syria's people have grown cotton, wheat, and other crops on its rich farmland. Today, however, Syria's farming methods are out-of-date. Many Syrians have moved to cities. President Bashar Assad has launched economic and political reforms to improve Syria's economy.

In the 1920s, Iraq began using money from newly discovered oil to modernize. In recent years, however, war has hurt the economy. In 1990 Iraq attacked Kuwait. In 1991 armed forces led by the United States and supported by the United Nations freed Kuwait. Iraq refused to accept UN terms for a cease-fire. The UN therefore placed an **embargo**, or strict limits on trade, on Iraq. The effects on Iraq's economy caused suffering for its people.

> ### THE **BIG** IDEA
>
> Jordan and Lebanon have been greatly affected by conflicts in Southwest Asia. Syria has rich farmland, and oil is important to Iraq.

◼ GRAPHIC SUMMARY: *Conflicts in Southwest Asia*

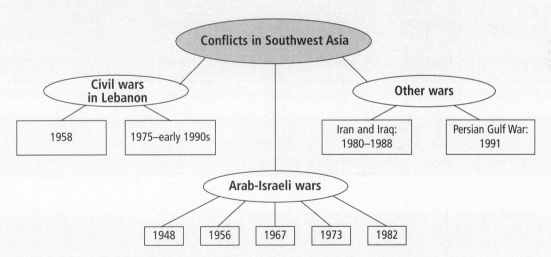

There have been many conflicts among the countries of Southwest Asia.

◼ REVIEW QUESTIONS

1. How did war hurt agriculture in Jordan?

2. Diagram Skills In what years were there Arab-Israeli wars?

ARABIAN PENINSULA

■ TEXT SUMMARY

The Arabian Peninsula has the world's largest sand desert, the Rub' al-Khali, or the Empty Quarter. The peninsula has no body of fresh water. But it has the world's largest known oil reserves.

Until oil was discovered in the 1930s, most people lived by fishing, trading, herding, and growing crops in the oases. Oil paid for modernization. Oil money built plants to remove the salt from seawater so it could be used for drinking and irrigation. This process is called **desalination**.

In 1960, Iran, Iraq, Kuwait, and Saudi Arabia joined with Venezuela to form the Organization of Petroleum Exporting Countries (OPEC). OPEC decides how much oil to produce and at what price to sell it. The countries of this region know that they will one day run out of oil and have invested money to develop other industries.

Saudi Arabia has spent billions of dollars to build its **infrastructure**. An infrastructure is a country's basic support facilities, such as schools, roads, airports, and communication systems.

Saudi Arabia has Islam's most sacred cities—Mecca and Medina. Each year two million Muslims from all over the world visit Saudi Arabia for the hajj, or religious journey to Mecca.

Oman and Yemen have changed little. They only recently began to develop oil resources. Yemen is the poorest country on the peninsula.

THE BIG IDEA

Oil made most countries on the Arabian Peninsula rich and helped them modernize. Oman and Yemen are the least developed countries in the region.

■ GRAPHIC SUMMARY: *Countries of the Arabian Peninsula*

COUNTRY	AREA (in square miles)	CAPITAL
Bahrain	266	Manama
Kuwait	6,880	Kuwait City
Oman	82,031	Muscat
Qatar	4,247	Doha
Saudi Arabia	829,996	Riyadh
United Arab Emirates	32,278	Abu Dhabi
Yemen	203,849	Sanaa

Source: Microsoft Encarta Interactive World Atlas 2000

The countries of the Arabian Peninsula vary greatly in size.

■ REVIEW QUESTIONS

1. Why are countries on the Arabian Peninsula investing money in other industries besides oil?

2. **Chart Skills** Which is the largest country in the Arabian Peninsula?

TURKEY, IRAN, AND CYPRUS

◼ TEXT SUMMARY

Although the majority of people in Turkey and Iran are Muslims, they are not Arabs.

Present-day Turkey consists of just a small part of the former Ottoman Empire. In 1923, Mustafa Kemal overthrew the sultan and made Turkey a republic. His goal was to make Turkey a modern country. He separated the Islamic religion and the government. The Turks gave him the name Atatürk, meaning "father of the Turks." Conflicts remain in Turkey about how much influence Islam should have.

Persians are the main cultural group in Iran. In 1925, army officer Reza Khan declared himself **shah**, or ruler. His son, Mohammad Reza Pahlavi, used profits from the oil industry to try to make Iran into a modern, Westernized nation. Religious leaders called **ayatollahs** wanted Iran to be ruled by strict Islamic law. They led a revolution in 1979 that forced the shah to flee. They declared Iran an Islamic republic and began getting rid of Western influences. Revolution and an eight-year war with Iraq hurt Iran's economy. Iran has begun to do away with some of its more extreme rules.

The population of Cyprus is four fifths Greek and one fifth Turkish. Civil war divided the island in the 1960s when some Greek Cypriots wanted to unite with Greece. Turkey sent troops to Cyprus and took control of the northeast, which has a majority Turkish population.

THE **BIG** IDEA

Turkey is a modern nation. An Islamic revolution in Iran hurt its economy. Cyprus is split by ethnic conflict.

◼ GRAPHIC SUMMARY:
The Countries of Southwest Asia

Country	Population	Life Expectancy (years)	Per Capita GDP (in US $)
Cyprus	748,982	76.8	10,990
Iran	68,959,931	68.3	1,530
Iraq	21,722,287	66.5	NA
Israel	3,619,480	78.4	16,810
Jordan	4,434,978	72.8	1,580
Kuwait	1,913,285	76.8	16,790
Lebanon	3,505,794	70.6	3,610
Oman	2,363,591	71.0	5,670
Saudi Arabia	20,785,955	70.0	7,000
Syria	16,673,282	67.8	1,200
Turkey	64,566,511	72.8	2,980
Yemen	16,387,963	59.5	350

Source: *Microsoft Encarta Interactive World Atlas 2000*

NA indicates data not available

The countries of Southwest Asia have great differences in life expectancy and per capita income.

◼ REVIEW QUESTIONS

1. How did Atatürk change Turkey?

2. Chart Skills Which country—Turkey, Iran, or Cyprus—has the largest population?

CHAPTER 23 *Test*

◼ IDENTIFYING MAIN IDEAS

Write the letter of the correct answer in the blank provided. (10 points each)

____ **1.** What happened to the Ottoman Empire after World War I?
  A. It was divided into many different countries.
  B. It grew into the world's largest empire.
  C. It spread across all of Southwest Asia.
  D. It became one large Arab country.

____ **2.** How did Arab countries react to Israel's independence?
  A. They welcomed Israel as a neighbor.
  B. They offered Israel a peace plan.
  C. They attacked Israel.
  D. They planned a conference.

____ **3.** How did the Israelis change the Negev Desert?
  A. They drained its swamps to create highways.
  B. They used irrigation to turn it into swamps.
  C. They used irrigation to turn it into fertile farmland.
  D. They turned it into a sea.

____ **4.** What did the Palestine Liberation Organization demand?
  A. that Palestine become the capital of Israel
  B. that Palestinians be allowed to live in any country
  C. that Palestinians be allowed to join the Israeli army
  D. that Palestine be freed

____ **5.** Lebanon's strong economy was destroyed by
  A. war with Iran.
  B. civil war between Greeks and Turks.
  C. civil wars among Muslim and Christian groups.
  D. an Islamic revolution.

____ **6.** What is an embargo?
  A. a large supply of oil
  B. strict limits on trade
  C. free trade
  D. a fertile farm

____ **7.** What has helped the Arabian Peninsula to modernize rapidly?
  A. money from oil
  B. money from the United States
  C. money from other Arab countries
  D. new factories

____ **8.** Mecca and Medina are Islam's most sacred cities. In which country are they located?
  A. Yemen
  B. Oman
  C. Kuwait
  D. Saudi Arabia

____ **9.** Who was Kemal Atatürk?
  A. the last sultan of Turkey
  B. the leader who made Turkey a modern republic
  C. the first shah of Turkey
  D. the Turkish leader who set up an Islamic republic

____ **10.** What happened as a result of Iran's revolution of 1979?
  A. Iran became an Islamic republic and its economy became weaker.
  B. Iran became an Islamic republic and its economy grew better.
  C. Iran became a democratic republic and ended Islamic law.
  D. Iran modernized and adopted European laws instead of Islamic laws.

Regional Atlas

INTRODUCTION TO AFRICA

■ TEXT SUMMARY

The first modern humans emerged from Africa over 100,000 years ago. African kingdoms arose and trade with Europe and Asia became common. The **Sahel**, the area just south of the Sahara, became an important trade region.

European countries colonized Africa, dividing the land without regard to existing divisions. By the 1960s, most African nations had achieved independence, but they have had difficulty uniting because they have maintained the borders imposed by Europeans.

Most of Africa consists of **plateaus**, or elevated blocks of land with flat or gently rolling surfaces. Mountains and **escarpments**, or steep cliffs, are found near coasts. The desert known as the Sahara is the primary geographic feature in the north. Waterfalls and cataracts along rivers make navigation from inland to the coasts difficult.

Rain falls in broad zones on either side of the Equator in Africa. Moving north and south, the land becomes drier as it turns to desert. The northern and southern edges of Africa have a Mediterranean climate. Africa's ecosystems have diverse wildlife.

South of the Sahara, more than 800 languages are spoken. Africa's most common economic activities are subsistence farming and **nomadic herding**, in which herders move their animals to different pastures throughout the year.

In many parts of Africa, the population is growing very rapidly and urbanization is increasing. Other parts have high death rates from disease that cancel out high birthrates.

THE **BIG** IDEA

Africa lies between the Atlantic Ocean on the west and the Indian Ocean on the east. The continent's location, as well as its varied landforms and climates, all play a role in shaping the lives of the many people of the region.

■ GRAPHIC SUMMARY:
Regions of Africa

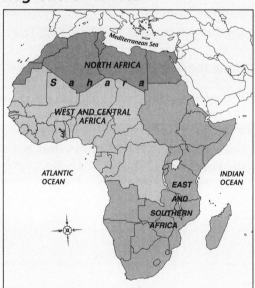

Africa is often divided into three distinct regions—North Africa, West and Central Africa, and East and Southern Africa.

■ REVIEW QUESTIONS

1. What is the Sahara?

2. **Map Skills** Which region has a coast on the Indian Ocean?

CHAPTER 24 *Test*

IDENTIFYING MAIN IDEAS

Write the letter of the correct answer in the blank provided. (10 points each)

_____ **1.** Africa's history can be traced back to
   A. the development of the slave trade.
   B. the origins of modern humans.
   C. the establishment of ancient kingdoms.
   D. the colonialism by Europeans.

_____ **2.** What is the Sahel?
   A. the area north of the Sahara
   B. the area south of the Sahara
   C. poor farmland of the rain forest
   D. rich farmland of the rain forest

_____ **3.** When Europeans colonized Africa in the 1800s, colonial borders were created based on
   A. agreements made by European nations.
   B. agreements made by African leaders.
   C. existing divisions.
   D. the physical features of the land.

_____ **4.** What is a plateau?
   A. desert land with few plants
   B. land below sea level
   C. a steep mountain
   D. elevated land with a flat or gently rolling surface

_____ **5.** Escarpments can be found
   A. in the desert.
   B. near the coast.
   C. in the Sahara.
   D. in fertile plains.

_____ **6.** Navigation on Africa's rivers is made difficult by
   A. narrow straits.
   B. shallow water.
   C. many waterfalls.
   D. rocky sandbars.

_____ **7.** In Africa
   A. several hundred languages are spoken.
   B. very few languages are spoken.
   C. there is complete ethnic unity.
   D. the land lacks mineral wealth.

_____ **8.** Africa's population lives mainly
   A. in urban areas.
   B. near bodies of water.
   C. along the Equator.
   D. in the Sahel.

_____ **9.** Africa's Mediterranean climate can be found
   A. near the east coast.
   B. around the Equator.
   C. in Madagascar.
   D. along the northern and southern tips.

_____ **10.** Nomadic herding is
   A. the hunting of wild animal herds.
   B. uncommon in Africa.
   C. traveling to different pastures during the year.
   D. often done in rain forests.

North Africa

SECTION 1 *EGYPT*

TEXT SUMMARY

Egypt's location in northeast Africa and its large size and population make it an important country. It is a land of deserts, except near the Nile River. The Nile is the longest river in the world.

About 99 percent of Egypt's people live near the Nile, where land is fertile. In rural villages, the way of life has changed slowly. Life in the fast-growing cities has changed quickly. Many people who move to the cities cannot find jobs or housing.

Egypt is more than 5,000 years old. Ancient Egyptians were among the first people in the world to set up an organized government and religion and to invent a written language. The famous pyramids of ancient Egypt were built as tombs for its pharaohs, or rulers. Arabs conquered Egypt in A.D. 642, bringing Islam and the Arabic language.

The Suez Canal, linking the Mediterranean and Red seas, was built in 1869. Britain controlled Egypt for many years until 1952 when the Egyptian army overthrew the government.

Egypt joined other Arab countries in wars against Israel. In 1979 Egypt became the first Arab country to make peace with Israel.

Until recently, the Nile flooded every year, providing Egyptians with water and fertile soil. Egypt built the Aswan High Dam to store water in a **reservoir**, or artificial lake. The dam and reservoir ended the flooding and now provide water and hydroelectric power throughout the year.

> ### THE **BIG** IDEA
>
> Most Egyptians live near the Nile River. Rapid growth of its population and cities have created challenges for Egypt.

GRAPHIC SUMMARY: *Egypt's Major Imports*

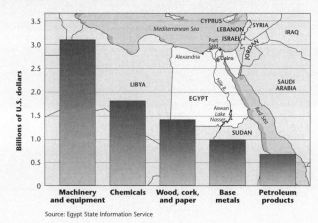

Source: Egypt State Information Service

Lacking investments to start new industries, Egypt must import most industrial products.

REVIEW QUESTIONS

1. Why do most Egyptians live near the Nile River?

2. Graph Skills What is Egypt's major import?

LIBYA AND THE MAGHREB

TEXT SUMMARY

Libya and the Maghreb countries—Tunisia, Algeria, and Morocco—are west of Egypt. The word *Maghreb* comes from the Arabic term meaning "land farthest west." Most people in this region are Muslims who speak Arabic. They live mainly along the Mediterranean coast. Inland from this narrow coast is the Sahara.

The Romans brought camels from central Asia. These animals, which can travel for days without water, allowed North Africans to trade with people south of the Sahara. Traders crossed the desert in **caravans**, large groups of merchants that traveled together for safety.

Arab armies invaded during the mid-600s. The region soon became a center of trade between Europe, Africa, and Asia. In the 1800s and early 1900s, France ruled Algeria, Tunisia, and Morocco and Italy conquered Libya.

Most farmers live in rural villages and have kept traditional ways of life. The cities are growing rapidly. People migrating from rural villages have trouble finding jobs and houses.

Oil was found in Libya in 1961 and soon became its main export. Oil money was used to modernize the country. Algeria's main export is also oil. But the government wants rural Algerians to continue farming to reduce the need to buy food from other countries.

Tunisia and Morocco do not have much oil. Both countries spend a lot on schools and on developing their manufacturing.

THE BIG IDEA

North Africa has been influenced by African, Arab, and European cultures. There are big differences between cities and rural areas.

GRAPHIC SUMMARY: *The Countries of North Africa*

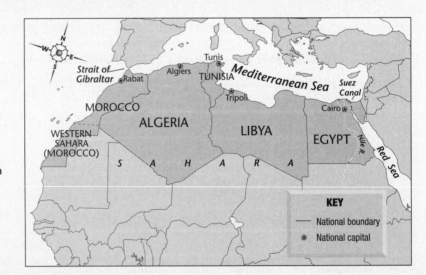

The countries of North Africa border the Mediterranean Sea.

REVIEW QUESTIONS

1. In which two countries is oil the major export?

2. Map Skills Which countries border Tunisia?

CHAPTER 25 *Test*

■ IDENTIFYING MAIN IDEAS

Write the letter of the correct answer in the blank provided. (10 points each)

____ 1. Where do most Egyptians live?
A. on the Mediterranean coast
B. near the Nile
C. in the desert
D. in the mountains

____ 2. What problem do Egypt's fast-growing cities have?
A. They cannot find enough people to work in their factories.
B. Not enough people are moving to cities from farms.
C. Nobody wants to live in the cities.
D. They are growing too fast to provide enough houses and jobs.

____ 3. Ancient Egyptians were among the first people to
A. speak Arabic.
B. develop a written language.
C. become Muslims.
D. use camels to cross the desert.

____ 4. What two bodies of water are connected by the Suez Canal?
A. the Mediterranean Sea and the Red Sea
B. the Red Sea and the Indian Ocean
C. the Indian Ocean and the Mediterranean Sea
D. the Mediterranean Sea and the Atlantic Ocean

____ 5. The Aswan High Dam
A. provided Egypt with hydroelectric power.
B. made farming possible in Egypt.
C. created the desert.
D. made Egypt's soil fertile.

____ 6. Which countries are included in the Maghreb?
A. Libya and Egypt
B. Egypt, Morocco, and Libya
C. Tunisia, Algeria, and Morocco
D. Libya, the Sudan, and Ethiopia

____ 7. What is a caravan?
A. a large group that travels together for safety
B. a family of camels in the desert
C. a show of riding skills on camels
D. any large group of Arabs

____ 8. Which country ruled Libya?
A. Maghreb
B. France
C. Egypt
D. Italy

____ 9. Where have most people kept traditional ways of life?
A. in rural villages
B. in cities
C. on the coasts
D. in none of these countries

____ 10. Which two countries of the Maghreb do not have much oil?
A. Libya and Algeria
B. Morocco and Tunisia
C. Tunisia and Algeria
D. Morocco and Libya

West and Central Africa

SECTION 1 *THE SAHEL*

■ TEXT SUMMARY

THE BIG IDEA

Ancient empires ruled the Sahel, an area between the Sahara and the tropical rain forest. Interaction between people and the environment in the Sahel has created serious problems. These countries are using their natural resources to try to be self-sufficient.

The Sahara was not always desert. As its climate grew drier, people moved north or south. Traders linked them, selling salt from the north for ivory, slaves, and gold from the south. Sahel rulers grew rich by taxing the traders. The region had three great empires—Ghana, Mali, and Songhai. (See chart below.)

Today, the northern Sahel has five countries—Mauritania, Mali (named for the ancient kingdom), Burkina Faso, Niger, and Chad. Many people are farmers. Because the soil is poor, they use **shifting agriculture**. They clear a part of the forest to grow crops. Then after the soil is no longer useful, farmers move on and clear another part of the forest. They grow millet and sorghum to eat and peanuts to sell. Others in the Sahel herd camels, cattle, and sheep.

Herding, shifting agriculture, and chopping firewood hurt the environment. Land stripped of trees suffers **deforestation**. When there is a drought, huge areas of the Sahel may lose all vegetation, which is called **desertification**. The savanna turns to desert.

As desertification increases, people leave for the cities. They join camps of **refugees**, people who flee to escape danger.

Aid from other countries has helped Sahel countries survive in their harsh environment. But these countries are also working to develop their natural resources—rivers and minerals—and people's skills.

■ GRAPHIC SUMMARY: *Ancient Empires of the Sahel*

Three great empires once ruled lands in the Sahel.

GHANA	MALI	SONGHAI
Ghana becomes a great kingdom in 400.	Mali is one of the largest empires in the world in the 1300s. Its most famous emperor, Mansa Musa, makes a journey to Mecca.	The Songhai Empire takes over as Mali declines.
By 800 Koumbi Saleh, the capital, has a very large population.	Tombouctou, the capital, is an important trading city and a center for Islamic arts and learning.	Under Mohammad Askia, Tombouctou reaches the height of its influence and learning.

■ REVIEW QUESTIONS

1. What is desertification?

2. **Chart Skills** Which empire ruled in the Sahel most recently?

THE COASTAL COUNTRIES

TEXT SUMMARY

The countries of this region, along the coast of West Africa, have advantages over the Sahel. They have a wetter climate and are located on the sea. They trade more with Europe than across the Sahara.

Most coastal countries export raw materials to other nations. Peanuts and cocoa beans are also exported.

The economies of the coastal countries suffer because they import more than they export. They have large debts because they borrowed money and now pay billions of dollars in interest.

When African countries gained independence, their economies were weak. Few countries have been able to recover from these economic problems. Most had weak governments, and the army seized power in **coups**, sudden political takeovers. One-man rule was common. Civil strife and warfare have often erupted in many West African nations, including Liberia and Sierra Leone.

Many West Africans have begun grass-roots efforts to improve the economy. People have taken it upon themselves to improve the economy instead of relying on the government for change. Women in particular have played an important role in these efforts. In many countries, women grow crops and work together to improve the economic conditions of their villages. They also organize food markets and have begun running small businesses. These efforts help to boost the depressed economy.

THE BIG IDEA

A good location has allowed the region to trade with Europe since the 1400s. Many countries have had shifts of power. Some are turning to democracy.

GRAPHIC SUMMARY: *The Coastal Countries*

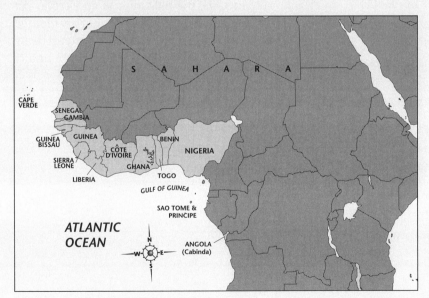

The coastal nations lie to the south of the countries of the Sahel.

REVIEW QUESTIONS

1. What is a coup?

2. **Map Skills** On what ocean are the coastal countries located?

■ TEXT SUMMARY

Nigeria was once seen as Africa's hope. Instead, poor leadership and lack of unity have caused problems. Nigeria is not united because it has many regions and ethnic groups. Vegetation includes coastal swamps, rain forests, savanna, and desert scrub. Climate varies from heavy rainfall to little rain.

Different groups control each area. The south has the best land. Yoruba took the southwest, and Ibo the southeast. Hausa and Fulani control the most fertile northern lands. Nigeria's middle region has the poorest soil and weakest groups. Nigeria's people often face problems because of religious or political differences.

Nigeria's main export is oil. The economy was good until oil prices fell in the early 1980s. Then military leaders overthrew the government in a coup. The new leaders asked the **World Bank** and the **International Monetary Fund** for help. Both are United Nations agencies that lend money to countries. Nigeria agreed to make the economic changes suggested by these agencies. Nigeria sold government-owned businesses to private companies, fired some government workers, and kept wages and prices down. People protested and called for free elections.

In 1993, the military held an election but threw out the results. The military remained in control, and political opponents were jailed or killed. Free elections were finally held in 1999, but Nigeria faces many challenges as it attempts to deal with its cultural and political disunity.

■ GRAPHIC SUMMARY:
The Coastal Countries

Country	Population	Life Expectancy (years)	Per Capita GDP (in US $)
Benin	6,100,799	53.6	370
Cape Verde	399,857	70.5	1,060
Côte d'Ivoire	15,446,231	46.2	720
Gambia	1,291,858	53.9	340
Ghana	18,497,206	56.8	380
Guinea	7,477,110	46.0	560
Guinea-Bissau	1,206,311	49.1	230
Liberia	2,771,901	59.5	NA
Nigeria	110,532,242	53.5	340
Senegal	9,723,149	57.4	520
Sierra Leone	5,080,004	48.6	170
Togo	4,905,827	58.8	340

Source: *Microsoft Encarta Interactive World Atlas 2000*
NA indicates data not available

Nigeria has the largest population in Africa.

■ REVIEW QUESTIONS

1. Why did Nigeria have to turn to the World Bank and the International Monetary Fund for help?

2. **Chart Skills** What is the population of Nigeria?

CENTRAL AFRICA

TEXT SUMMARY

The countries of Central Africa range from the tiny island nation of São Tomé and Príncipe to the Democratic Republic of the Congo, the largest country south of the Sahara.

The largest river of the region is the Congo. This river system is a highway providing food, water, and transportation. A thick rain forest in the Congo Basin limits movement. Its valuable wood can be cut and exported only near rivers or railroads. Both the savanna and rain forest have poor soil. Large numbers of people have moved to Kinshasa, the capital.

Across the Congo River from Kinshasa is Brazzaville, capital of the Congo Republic. Its railroad serves the inland countries of Chad and the Central African Republic.

Many countries of West and Central Africa belong to an economic community known as the CFA. They use a form of money called the CFA franc.

Central African countries have many mineral resources. The Democratic Republic of the Congo has copper, cobalt, and diamonds. But the country's problems have kept them from being mined.

After independence in 1960, the Democratic Republic of the Congo was torn apart by Belgian troops, United Nations forces, rebel armies, and hired soldiers called **mercenaries**. A general by the name of Mobutu Sese Seko became dictator. The nation fell deeply into debt, and in 1997 Mobutu's rule was overthrown.

THE BIG IDEA

Rivers, forests, and grasslands affect movement in Central Africa. Misuse of rivers and forests hurts the environment.

GRAPHIC SUMMARY: *The Countries of Central Africa*

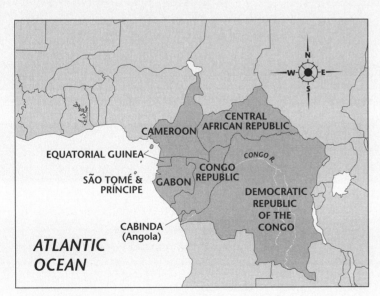

The countries of Central Africa extend inland from the Atlantic Ocean.

REVIEW QUESTIONS

1. Why is the Congo River important to the region?

2. Map Skills Which Central African country does not have a seacoast?

CHAPTER 26 *Test*

◼ IDENTIFYING MAIN IDEAS

Write the letter of the correct answer in the blank provided. (10 points each)

____ 1. Farmers who use shifting agriculture have to
  A. move often because the soil is no longer useful.
  B. remain in one place because the soil gets more fertile.
  C. pay high rent to the landowners.
  D. use modern tools to grow crops.

____ 2. Ghana, Mali, and Songhai were
  A. countries in the Sahel.
  B. countries with large debts.
  C. empires in Central Africa.
  D. empires in the Sahel.

____ 3. What advantage do coastal countries have over the Sahel?
  A. easier trade across the Sahara
  B. a wetter climate and a seacoast
  C. no large debts
  D. stronger governments

____ 4. What is a coup?
  A. a sudden political takeover
  B. a democratic election
  C. a weak economy
  D. an important mineral export

____ 5. Why are women an important part of the economy in West Africa?
  A. They run most of the banks.
  B. They own the factories and mines.
  C. They grow crops and run food markets.
  D. They are the political leaders.

____ 6. Nigeria has had problems because of poor leadership and
  A. high oil prices.
  B. too few people.
  C. no national unity.
  D. no international loans.

____ 7. Nigeria's main export is
  A. peanuts.
  B. manufactured goods.
  C. oil.
  D. cocoa beans.

____ 8. What happened after the 1993 election in Nigeria?
  A. A democratic government took over.
  B. All political prisoners were let out of jail.
  C. Nigeria paid off all its debts.
  D. The military threw out the results.

____ 9. What is the largest African country south of the Sahara?
  A. Democratic Republic of the Congo
  B. Algeria
  C. São Tomé and Príncipe
  D. Nigeria

____ 10. What is the CFA franc?
  A. a favorite food in Africa
  B. the postage stamp used by the Central African Republic
  C. the money used by several countries in West and Central Africa
  D. a railroad that carries goods to the coast

East and Southern Africa

 **SECTION 1** *KENYA*

TEXT SUMMARY

Kenya is known for its national parks where wild animals roam freely and are protected. It is located on the east coast of Africa. The Equator runs through Kenya, and some places are very hot. The Great Rift Valley crosses the highlands, where elevation makes the climate cooler.

Most people live in the fertile highlands of the southwest, which have forests, grasslands, and enough rain to grow crops. When the British took control of Kenya in the early 1890s, they built a railroad west from the coast. They encouraged whites to settle in the highlands. Africans, especially Masai and Kikuyu, lost their land.

In the 1950s, the Kikuyu fought the British settlers. The British crushed the uprising. But a Kikuyu leader, Jomo Kenyatta, became president when Kenya gained independence. He returned some land to the Kikuyu.

Kenyatta encouraged **harambee**, "pulling together." He wanted the government, private companies, and individuals to work to create a strong economy. The government encouraged farmers to grow cash crops—coffee and tea. That left little farmland for food, forcing Kenya to import food. Many people suffer from **malnutrition**, a disease caused by an unhealthy diet.

Kenya began to face hard times in the 1980s. It could not provide its fast-growing population with enough food or jobs. Ethnic conflict replaced *harambee*. Kenya has been ruled by one party for many years. Kenyans hope to return their country to fair elections and unity.

> ### THE **BIG** IDEA
>
> After independence, Kenyans worked together to build a strong economy. But today Kenya is struggling to keep its economy strong and its people united.

GRAPHIC SUMMARY:
Countries of East Africa

Country	Population	Life Expectancy (years)	Per Capita GDP (in US $)
Burundi	5,537,387	45.6	730
Djibouti	440,727	51.1	1,200
Eritrea	3,842,436	55.3	750
Ethiopia	58,390,351	40.9	560
Kenya	28,337,071	47.6	1,600
Rwanda	7,956,172	41.9	720
Somalia	6,841,695	46.2	600
Sudan	33,550,552	56.0	940
Tanzania	30,608,769	46.4	550
Uganda	22,167,195	42.6	1,060

Source: *Microsoft Encarta Interactive World Atlas 2000*

Most of the people of the region have a short life expectancy.

REVIEW QUESTIONS

1. What is *harambee* and how did it help Kenya?

2. Chart Skills In which one of these countries do people have the longest life expectancy?

OTHER COUNTRIES OF EAST AFRICA

◼ TEXT SUMMARY

THE **BIG** IDEA

Several countries in the region have important locations. Conflicts have badly hurt some countries in East Africa.

Ethiopia, Eritrea, Djibouti, and Somalia are located on a landform known as the Horn of Africa. They are near the oil supplies of the Middle East and the shipping lanes of the Red Sea and the Gulf of Aden.

Several countries have been torn by civil wars, wars with each other, and the effects of severe droughts. Ethiopia had to allow the province of Eritrea to become independent in 1993. Civil war and drought caused a terrible famine in Somalia. The people of the Sudan are divided. Arab Muslims live in the north. People in the south belong to several African ethnic groups and practice African religions or Christianity. North and south have fought since independence in 1956.

Uganda, Rwanda, and Burundi are landlocked, or entirely surrounded by land. Uganda is recovering from a civil war and a ruthless dictator. It is becoming more democratic.

Rwanda and Burundi are each ruled by an **ethnocracy**—a government controlled by one ethnic group. In Rwanda, the Hutu majority murdered great numbers of Tutsi in 1994. About 2 million Rwandans became refugees. Burundi is controlled by the Tutsi, although they are a minority. Many thousands of Hutu have been killed by Tutsi.

Tanzania has fertile land and mineral wealth but remains very poor. Tanzania's economy failed when people were subjected to **villagization**—forced to work on collective farms. After Tanzania abandoned this policy, the economy began to improve.

◼ GRAPHIC SUMMARY:
The Countries of East Africa

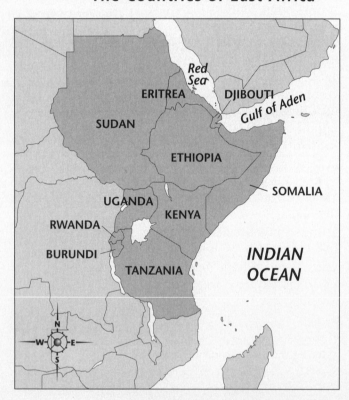

Several countries in the region have strategic locations on water routes. Others are landlocked.

◼ REVIEW QUESTIONS

1. Which country was once a province of Ethiopia?

2. **Map Skills** What bodies of water are east and north of the Horn of Africa?

SOUTH AFRICA

TEXT SUMMARY

The Republic of South Africa is the wealthiest country in Africa. Although three quarters of the population is black, a white minority ruled for most of the 1900s. Whites also controlled the land, jobs, and gold and diamond mines.

The Dutch were the first Europeans to settle in South Africa. Their descendants, called Boers or Afrikaners, speak Afrikaans. The British followed and defeated the Afrikaners. The Africans were forced into separate lands or made to work for low pay.

South Africa became independent in 1961 and passed laws to keep black Africans from moving to the cities. Each African was assigned to a region called a homeland. Africans needed a pass to live somewhere else. The whites also passed a system of laws called **apartheid**, which means "apartness." Apartheid laws **segregated** black South Africans, or forced them to live separately.

Apartheid and the homelands were so unjust that other countries protested. In 1986, the United States and other countries placed **sanctions** against South Africa. Sanctions punish a country for behaving in a way that other nations do not approve.

In 1989, a new prime minister named F. W. de Klerk promised reform. Black leader Nelson Mandela was released from jail after 27 years. All apartheid laws were ended. In 1994, Mandela was elected the country's first black president. South Africa adopted a new constitution guaranteeing equal rights for all South Africans.

THE BIG IDEA

For most of the 1900s, a white minority controlled South Africa. In the 1990s, the apartheid system was abolished. South Africa now has a new, democratic constitution.

GRAPHIC SUMMARY: *The End of Apartheid*

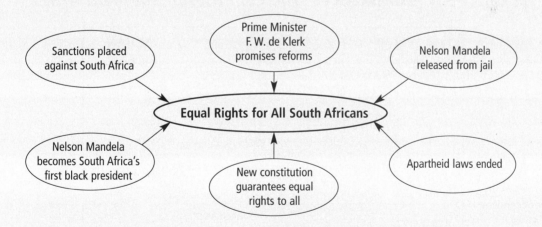

After years of white rule, all South Africans are now guaranteed equal rights.

REVIEW QUESTIONS

1. What is apartheid?

2. Diagram Skills Name two actions that led to equal rights for all South Africans.

OTHER COUNTRIES OF SOUTHERN AFRICA

▨ TEXT SUMMARY

THE BIG IDEA

All the countries of southern Africa are affected by South Africa.

South Africa is so powerful that it affects all of southern Africa. Lesotho is an **enclave** of South Africa. An enclave is completely surrounded by a larger country. The economies of Lesotho and Swaziland depend on South Africa. Until recently, Namibia was controlled by South Africa. Many people from Malawi are migrant workers in South Africa. Botswana sells diamonds, copper, coal, and beef cattle.

Angola and Mozambique became independent in 1975 after long wars with Portugal. Both countries adopted Communist economic systems. Rebel groups, helped by South Africa, fought these governments for many years. Their economies fell apart and disease and malnutrition became common. Angola held its first free election in 1992, although

fighting has continued. War ended in Mozambique, and its economy has improved. However, in 2000 floods devastated much of the land.

Zambia's government counted on money from the export of copper to buy food. When the price of copper dropped, Zambia did not have enough money to feed all its people. Today its economy is still trying to recover.

Before full independence, Zimbabwe's white minority had control of the government, as well as most of the nation's fertile land and wealth. This caused conflict with the black majority. Although full independence came in 1980, racial conflicts ignited once again. White-owned farmland was forcibly taken away and given to black farmers. Violent protest erupted and the government repressed many of the people's democratic freedoms.

▨ GRAPHIC SUMMARY: *The Countries of Southern Africa*

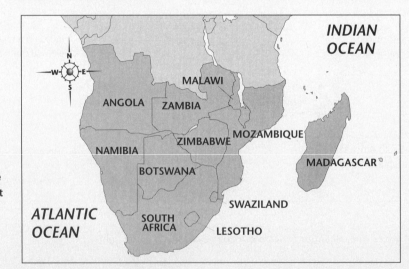

Most countries in the region are dependent on South Africa.

▨ REVIEW QUESTIONS

1. How did Zambia's dependence on copper exports create a problem?

2. **Map Skills** Which countries in the region have borders with South Africa?

CHAPTER 27 *Test*

▨ IDENTIFYING MAIN IDEAS

Write the letter of the correct answer in the blank provided. (10 points each)

_____ 1. Why does much of Kenya have a cool climate even though it is on the Equator?
A. The elevation keeps Kenya's lowland area cool.
B. Winds from the south bring cool air to Kenya.
C. The elevation keeps Kenya's highland area cool.
D. Kenya's river system cools the air.

_____ 2. What is *harambee*?
A. a system of growing cash crops
B. working together
C. a new kind of grain
D. a one-party government

_____ 3. What problems do many countries in East Africa face?
A. too much seacoast
B. too few ethnic groups
C. too much farmland
D. civil wars and famine

_____ 4. What is an ethnocracy?
A. a government controlled by one ethnic group
B. a study of all the ethnic groups in a country
C. a system of getting ethnic groups to work together
D. a fair distribution of government jobs among ethnic groups

_____ 5. What helped cause Tanzania's poverty?
A. It had no fertile land.
B. It had no mineral wealth.
C. It forced people to work on collective farms.
D. Most of its people fled the country.

_____ 6. What percentage of South Africa's population is black?
A. 25 percent
B. 50 percent
C. 60 percent
D. 75 percent

_____ 7. South Africa's apartheid laws
A. segregated black South Africans.
B. created jobs for everyone.
C. gave black South Africans homes in cities.
D. redistributed land.

_____ 8. What are sanctions?
A. laws that allow free trade
B. free and fair elections
C. discussions between countries
D. acts to punish a country for its behavior

_____ 9. Which country is an enclave of South Africa?
A. Swaziland
B. Angola
C. Malawi
D. Lesotho

_____ 10. Why did Zambia have a problem with copper exports?
A. When the price of copper rose, Zambia could not produce enough copper.
B. When the price of copper fell, Zambia did not have enough money to buy food.
C. Zambia did not have enough money to buy copper.
D. Zambia's mines ran out of copper.

INTRODUCTION TO SOUTH ASIA

◼ TEXT SUMMARY

THE **BIG** IDEA

The Himalayas formed a barrier that allowed the people of South Asia to develop their own unique cultures. South Asia is one of the most densely populated regions of the world.

The Indus Valley civilization, one of the world's oldest civilizations, began in South Asia. The region was invaded many times throughout history. The invaders introduced new ideas and beliefs to the region, which became influential in the shaping of South Asia's culture.

South Asia is a **subcontinent**, or large landmass forming a distinct part of a continent, in the southern part of Asia. The Himalayas, a mountain system with many of the world's highest mountains, separate South Asia from the rest of Asia.

Climate within the region depends on altitude and distance from the Indian Ocean. Portions of the region are seasonally affected by **monsoons**, winds that bring dry air in winter and rain in summer. Other areas, like the Thar Desert, receive very little precipitation.

South Asia's various ecosystems support its plentiful and diverse wildlife. However, poaching and the loss of habitat threaten several species.

South Asia has one of the most densely settled populations on earth. The population is becoming more urban as more people move to the cities in search of work. Many languages are spoken in South Asia, but about half the population of India speaks Hindi. The dominant religions are Hinduism and Islam, except in Bhutan, where Buddhism is the dominant religion.

Agriculture dominates South Asia's economy. Faced with an ever-increasing population, however, South Asia has had difficulty producing enough food. A large film industry boosts the economy of India. In some areas, women have found economic opportunity in the technological and business fields.

◼ GRAPHIC SUMMARY:
South Asia Monsoons

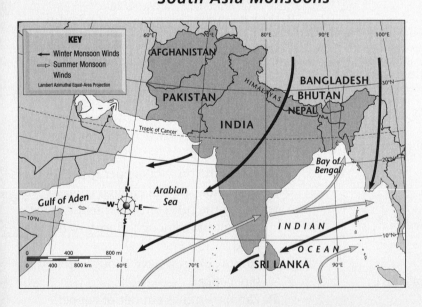

KEY
← Winter Monsoon Winds
⇨ Summer Monsoon Winds
Lambert Azimuthal Equal-Area Projection

AFGHANISTAN
PAKISTAN
HIMALAYAS
INDIA
Tropic of Cancer
BANGLADESH
BHUTAN
NEPAL
Bay of Bengal
Arabian Sea
Gulf of Aden
INDIAN OCEAN
SRI LANKA

Winter monsoons bring dry air.
Summer monsoons bring moisture and rain from the Indian Ocean.

◼ REVIEW QUESTIONS

1. What landform separates South Asia from the rest of Asia?

2. Map Skills Does the east coast or west coast of India get the summer monsoon rains?

CHAPTER 28 *Test*

◼ IDENTIFYING MAIN IDEAS

Write the letter of the correct answer in the blank provided. (10 points each)

_____ **1.** What is a subcontinent?
   A. an island near a continent
   B. any area that is cut off by mountains
   C. a large landmass forming a distinct part of a continent
   D. a continent surrounded by water

_____ **2.** South Asia's climate depends on
   A. altitude and distance from the Indian Ocean.
   B. the Himalayas, which block all precipitation.
   C. the temperature of the Indian Ocean.
   D. China's climate.

_____ **3.** Why are some South Asian species threatened?
   A. New animal species have killed off native species.
   B. Poaching and loss of habitat threaten many plants and animals.
   C. The monsoon winds have destroyed many plant species.
   D. South Asia relies on animal hunting for its economy.

_____ **4.** Why are so many people in South Asia moving to cities?
   A. to leave the crowded farmland
   B. to go to school
   C. to find work
   D. to escape civil wars

_____ **5.** About how much of the Indian population speaks Hindi?
   A. one third
   B. one half
   C. one fifth
   D. one fourth

_____ **6.** The major religions of South Asia are
   A. Hinduism and Islam.
   B. Christianity and Judaism.
   C. Buddhism and Christianity.
   D. Hinduism and Judaism.

_____ **7.** What are monsoons?
   A. religious leaders of South India
   B. seasonal winds that bring rains in summer and dry air in winter
   C. animals found only in South Asia
   D. any method of preventing floods

_____ **8.** The Himalayas separate South Asia from
   A. the monsoons.
   B. Africa.
   C. the rest of Asia.
   D. the Indian Ocean.

_____ **9.** What is the major economic activity of South Asia?
   A. livestock grazing
   B. manufacturing and trade
   C. fishing
   D. agriculture

_____ **10.** Women in South Asia are offered more economic opportunity in the fields of
   A. technology and business.
   B. engineering and manufacturing.
   C. fishing and livestock raising.
   D. textiles and entertainment.

The Countries of South Asia

 **SECTION 1** *ROAD TO INDEPENDENCE*

■ TEXT SUMMARY

On August 15, 1947, India became independent from Britain. British rule of India began in the mid-1700s. The colonial rulers ended slavery, improved schools, and built railroads. Other changes, however, hurt India. The British tried to end India's textile industry so they could sell British cloth in India. Indians were not allowed to hold high government and army positions.

In the late 1800s, Indians developed a strong feeling of **nationalism**, or pride in one's nation. Mohandas Gandhi led an independence movement. Gandhi encouraged **nonviolent resistance**—opposing an enemy by any means except violence. One method was to **boycott**—refuse to buy or use—British cloth. The sale of British cloth in India fell sharply.

For a while Hindus and Muslims worked together for independence. But as their goal got closer, conflicts between the two religious groups grew stronger. In 1947, the leaders agreed to **partition**, or divide, the subcontinent into separate Hindu and Muslim countries. The two new countries were the mostly Hindu India and the mostly Muslim Pakistan.

At independence, 12 million people moved on the subcontinent. Hindus moved to India and Muslims moved to Pakistan. About one million people were killed in fighting between Hindus and Muslims.

India and Pakistan have fought three wars. After the third war, in 1971, part of Pakistan became the independent country of Bangladesh.

> ### THE **BIG** IDEA
>
> **Mohandas Gandhi led a nonviolent struggle to gain independence for India from Britain. When India became independent it was divided into two countries—India and Pakistan.**

■ GRAPHIC SUMMARY: *Religions in South Asia*

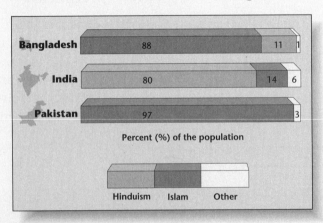

	Percent (%) of the population
Bangladesh	88 / 11 / 1
India	80 / 14 / 6
Pakistan	97 / 3

Hinduism   Islam   Other

Almost all people of India, Pakistan, and Bangladesh are Hindus or Muslims.

Source: *The World Almanac and Book of Facts, 2001*

■ REVIEW QUESTIONS

1. What is nonviolent resistance?

2. Graph Skills What percentage of Indians are Hindus?

INDIA'S PEOPLE AND ECONOMY

◼ TEXT SUMMARY

Most Indians are Hindus. Hindu society is based on the **caste system**. This is a social system in which each person is born into a caste, or group. Each caste has its own duties. Caste determines the work people do. At the top of the caste system are Brahmans—priests, teachers, and judges. (See graph below.) Untouchables have the lowest rank and do work that is thought to be "unclean."

About seven out of ten Indians live in farming villages. Many people own bicycles, but few own cars. Many villages now have electricity. Television, radio, and movies are important for spreading new ideas because many people cannot read. As people have moved to towns and cities, urban areas have become very crowded. People believe they have more opportunity in a city than in a village.

India's government is trying to raise the standard of living for people in both cities and villages. A major goal has been to feed the growing population. Increased irrigation and better farming methods have produced more and better crops. Many farmers have set up **cottage industries** to earn more money. People in cottage industries make goods at home.

India has become one of the world's leading industrial countries. It has made advances in computers and space research. There is a growing middle class. About half the people can read and write, and this percentage is growing. However, many people live on the streets or in slums.

THE **BIG** IDEA

Most Indians live in rural villages and follow traditional ways. Cities have a growing middle class. The government is working to improve the country's standard of living.

◼ GRAPHIC SUMMARY: *The Caste System*

Hindus are born into castes, which help determine how they live.

BRAHMANS
(priests, teachers, judges)

KSHATRIYAS
(warriors)

VAISYAS
(farmers and merchants)

SUDRAS
(craftworkers and laborers)

UNTOUCHABLES, OR OUTCASTS
(street sweepers, garbage collectors, and hide tanners)

◼ REVIEW QUESTIONS

1. Why are many Indians moving to cities?

2. **Diagram Skills** What are the main jobs of the Vaisyas?

OTHER COUNTRIES OF SOUTH ASIA

▦ TEXT SUMMARY

Each of India's neighbors has its own physical and cultural identity. In Pakistan, the Hindu Kush mountain range towers along its northern and western borders. The Baluchistan Plateau covers much of western Pakistan. To the east is the Thar Desert. Most Pakistanis live in the fertile valley of the Indus River. Most are farmers. The river provides **hydroelectric power** —electricity produced by the movement of the water—and **irrigates** the land, supplying water to dry areas. Islam links Pakistanis together, but ethnic conflicts divide them.

Mountainous Afghanistan has fertile valleys at the foot of the Hindu Kush. Semiarid plains lie to the north. As in Pakistan, Islam is the religion of almost all

the people. In 1979, the Soviet Union invaded Afghanistan. About 3 million Afghans fled. In 1989, the Soviets withdrew, but fighting among Afghan groups continued.

Bangladesh has fertile soil, but floods happen regularly. In good times, farmers harvest three crops a year. In bad times, overflowing rivers and tropical storms flood the land. Bangladesh is working to control flooding and overpopulation.

Nepal and Bhutan are in the Himalayas. Each has hot, humid southern lowlands with monsoon rains. Mount Everest, the world's highest mountain, is in Nepal.

Sri Lanka is an island country in the Indian Ocean. The majority of its people are Sinhalese, who control the government. A smaller group, the Tamils, have been fighting for independence.

> ### THE **BIG** IDEA
>
> **Water—too little or too much—has a major effect on Pakistan and Bangladesh. Other countries in the region have been shaped by their physical geography.**

▦ GRAPHIC SUMMARY: *The Countries of South Asia*

Country	Population	Life Expectancy (years)	Per Capita GDP (in US $)
Afghanistan	24,792,375	46.8	NA
Bangladesh	127,567,002	56.7	340
Bhutan	1,908,307	52.3	520
India	984,003,683	62.9	400
Nepal	23,698,421	57.9	220
Pakistan	135,135,195	59.1	480
Sri Lanka	18,933,558	72.5	810

The countries of South Asia differ greatly in size and income.

Source: *Microsoft Encarta Interactive World Atlas 2000*
NA indicates data not available.

▦ REVIEW QUESTIONS

1. Why is the Indus River important to Pakistan?

2. Chart Skills Which South Asian country has the highest per capita GDP?

CHAPTER 29 *Test*

■ IDENTIFYING MAIN IDEAS

Write the letter of the correct answer in the blank provided. (10 points each)

____ 1. Who was Mohandas Gandhi?
   A. the leader of India's independence movement
   B. the head of India's textile industry
   C. the leader of the group that used violence to gain independence
   D. a high official of the British government

____ 2. An example of nonviolent resistance would be
   A. forming an army to fight the enemy.
   B. kidnapping and killing one's enemies.
   C. giving in to the enemy to avoid violence.
   D. refusing to buy or use an enemy's products.

____ 3. What countries were created by the 1947 partition of British India?
   A. India, Pakistan, and Afghanistan
   B. Pakistan and Bangladesh
   C. India and Pakistan
   D. India, Pakistan, Nepal, and Bhutan

____ 4. How is a person's life affected by the caste system in India?
   A. People's lives are no longer affected at all by the caste system.
   B. The caste system helps people do whatever they want in life.
   C. Caste determines people's work and their rules for living.
   D. Caste determines if an Indian has the right to vote.

____ 5. People in India who cannot read get information from
   A. newspapers and magazines.
   B. radio and television.
   C. messengers on bicycles.
   D. the Internet.

____ 6. Why do many people in India move from farm villages to cities?
   A. There is more opportunity in cities.
   B. Cities have more space than villages.
   C. Hardly any villages have electricity.
   D. They do not want to use farm machinery.

____ 7. In what kinds of industry is India making great advances?
   A. hand weaving
   B. computers and space research
   C. automobiles and trucks
   D. televisions and radios

____ 8. Where in Pakistan do most people live?
   A. in the Baluchistan Plateau
   B. in the Thar Desert
   C. in the Indus River valley
   D. in the Hindu Kush

____ 9. What country invaded Afghanistan in 1979?
   A. Great Britain
   B. the Soviet Union
   C. India
   D. Pakistan

____ 10. In what country is Mount Everest located?
   A. India
   B. Sri Lanka
   C. Bhutan
   D. Nepal

INTRODUCTION TO EAST ASIA AND THE PACIFIC WORLD

◾ TEXT SUMMARY

THE BIG IDEA

This huge region includes countries on the continent of Asia as well as many island nations. The continents of Australia and Antarctica are also included.

East Asia is located where the Pacific and Indian oceans meet. Its location made it a great trading area for centuries. The geography of Southeast Asia consists mainly of mountains, river valleys, peninsulas, and islands. Australia is flat with broad deserts and low mountains.

Rain falls seasonally across much of the region. Monsoons occur in the tropical climates near the Equator. Australia is mostly arid and semiarid, though southern Australia and New Zealand have Mediterranean and marine west-coast climates.

Many plants and animals are found in the ecosystems of the region. Tropical rain forests line the coasts of northern Australia and East and Southeast Asia. Parts of East Asia, Australia, and New Zealand are deciduous forests; the interiors of China, Mongolia, and Australia are grasslands.

East Asia is heavily populated, with about 2 billion inhabitants. China's population alone is over 1 billion, with a third of them living in rural areas. Many ethnic, religious, and language groups live in the region. This has led to great cultural diversity.

The economies of the nations within the region contrast sharply with each other. While Japan and Australia are highly industrialized, China and much of Southeast Asia are focused on agriculture, where **intensive farming**—farming that requires much labor to produce food—is done. In hilly areas, farmers create **terraces**, flat ledges of land, like steps, to plant their crops.

◾ GRAPHIC SUMMARY: *East Asia and the Pacific*

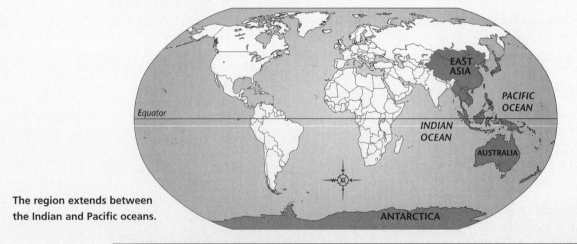

The region extends between the Indian and Pacific oceans.

◾ REVIEW QUESTIONS

1. What is intensive farming?

2. **Map Skills** Where are Australia and Antarctica located in relation to East Asia?

CHAPTER 30 *Test*

■ IDENTIFYING MAIN IDEAS

Write the letter of the correct answer in the blank provided. (10 points each)

____ **1.** What two oceans are found in East Asia?
   A. Atlantic and Pacific
   B. Pacific and Indian
   C. Indian and Atlantic
   D. Pacific and Arctic

____ **2.** Australia's landscape can be described as
   A. mountainous with many snow-covered peaks.
   B. flat with deserts and low mountains.
   C. river valleys with ample vegetation.
   D. a peninsula with many rivers.

____ **3.** What type of climate region can be found in the interior of China and Mongolia?
   A. desert scrub
   B. rain forests
   C. grasslands
   D. highlands

____ **4.** About how much of China's population is rural?
   A. one half
   B. one fourth
   C. two thirds
   D. one third

____ **5.** East Asia and the Pacific world have
   A. very few ethnic groups.
   B. only one main religion.
   C. diverse language groups.
   D. a population of 1 billion.

____ **6.** China's climate is
   A. similar to the climate of the United States.
   B. not at all like the climate of the United States.
   C. the same throughout China.
   D. different in every part of China.

____ **7.** What kind of climate does most of Southeast Asia have?
   A. arid
   B. semiarid
   C. continental
   D. tropical

____ **8.** The economies of China and Southeast Asia are mostly based on
   A. agriculture.
   B. manufacturing.
   C. commercial fishing.
   D. nomadic herding.

____ **9.** What is a terrace?
   A. a restaurant where farmers eat lunch
   B. an area where farmers burn crops
   C. a flat ledge of land farmers make to allow farming in hilly areas
   D. a vast plain that is good for farming

____ **10.** Australia's climate is mostly
   A. wet and tropical.
   B. arid and semiarid.
   C. subarctic.
   D. tropical wet and dry.

CHAPTER 31 China

SECTION 1 THE EMERGENCE OF MODERN CHINA

▣ TEXT SUMMARY

THE BIG IDEA

Mao Zedong made China a Communist nation. The Four Modernizations changed the economy. The government responded with violence to the call for democratic reforms.

Chinese civilization was born around 3000 B.C. Feeding China's large population has required large amounts of rice and other crops. By 1900, some European countries and the United States had divided China into **spheres of influence**. Countries had political and economic control in these areas but did not govern them directly.

In 1911, Chinese Nationalists forced the emperor to **abdicate**, or give up his throne. China was declared a republic. In the 1920s, the Nationalists attacked supporters of Communist ideas. In 1934, the Communists, led by Mao Zedong, fled to the mountains, beginning the Long March.

Japan invaded China in the 1930s. Nationalists and Communists cooperated to fight Japan but fought again after World War II. By 1949, the Communists won and Mao Zedong established the People's Republic of China.

Mao started the Great Leap Forward. Chinese peasants were forced to work on huge collective farms. Communist officials made all economic decisions. When production fell, Mao called for a Cultural Revolution to destroy the old order. These actions ruined the economy and destroyed many people's lives.

The next leader, Deng Xiaoping, started the Four Modernizations—improving agriculture, industry, science and technology, and defense. Farmers could rent land and sell extra crops for profit. Farm production increased.

Economic improvement led people to want freedom and democracy. In 1989, thousands demonstrated in Tiananmen Square in Beijing. Troops killed over 1,000 people.

▣ GRAPHIC SUMMARY: *China's Nationalists and Communists*

In the 1900s, there have been many attempts to change China.

| 1911 Nationalists over-throw the emperor | 1937–1945 Nationalists and Communists cooperate to fight Japan | 1958 Great Leap Forward begins | 1976 Four Modernizations begin |

1900　　1920　　1940　　1960　　1980

| 1934 Communists begin the Long March | 1949 Communists win control of China | 1966 Cultural Revolution begins | 1989 Troops kill demonstrators in Tiananmen Square |

▣ REVIEW QUESTIONS

1. What were the results of the Great Leap Forward and the Cultural Revolution?

2. Time Line Skills When did Nationalists and Communists cooperate?

REGIONS OF CHINA

◼ TEXT SUMMARY

For centuries, China's core was in the Northeast region. It contains Beijing, the country's capital, and the greatest concentrations of China's population.

Considered one of China's major industrial areas, the Northeast is also a farm region, made fertile by loess, a yellow soil carried by the Huang He. This river is a transportation route. It was called "China's Sorrow" because of destructive floods. Now people use so much of its water that it dries up for months.

The Southeast is warmer, wetter, and more mountainous than the Northeast. The Southeast, once China's main agricultural region, has become its economic center. The Yangzi River is a major east-west route. Shanghai, at its mouth, is China's major port and largest city. Four Special Economic Zones, set up to attract foreign money and technology, have made this region economically strong.

China's Northwest region is rugged and barren, with a small population. The Gobi Desert forms China's northern boundary. Herding is the main economic activity. The Silk Road, an ancient trade route, crossed this region. Stopping places at oases became towns.

The Plateau of Tibet dominates the Southwest and is the world's highest region. Tibet's farmers and herders are Buddhists led by a **theocrat**—a person who claims to rule by religious or divine authority—called the Dalai Lama. China invaded Tibet in 1950, destroying Buddhist monasteries and driving the Dalai Lama into exile. It tried to destroy Tibet's culture and designated the area as an **autonomous region**, a political unit with limited self-government. However, most Tibetans maintained their traditions and beliefs.

Most of China's people live in the two eastern regions.

THE **BIG** IDEA

Each of China's four main regions has its own character and is defined largely by geography.

◼ GRAPHIC SUMMARY:
The Four Regions of China

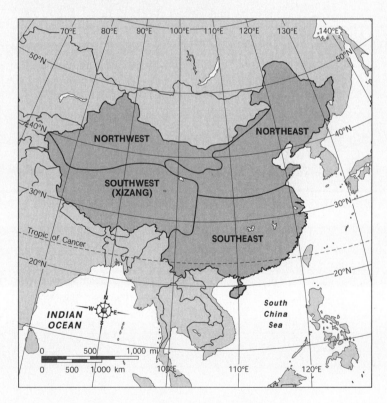

◼ REVIEW QUESTIONS

1. Which region was considered China's core for centuries?

2. Map Skills Name the regions of China.

CHINA'S PEOPLE AND CULTURE

■ TEXT SUMMARY

With 1.3 billion people, China has the world's largest population. Most Chinese share a common culture and written language.

Mao Zedong thought that China needed a large population. He urged people to have more children. By the mid-1960s, China had more people than it could feed or house.

When Deng Xiaoping took over, he said China had to reduce its population growth. He wanted each couple to have just one child. China rewarded families who had only one child with better housing, jobs, and pay. Couples who had more children faced fines, pay cuts, and loss of jobs. City dwellers usually followed this policy, but rural dwellers, who needed larger families to help in the fields, did not.

China has about 56 ethnic minorities, who live mostly in the west. But more than 1 billion people—92 percent—belong to the Han ethnic group. The Chinese speak different dialects, but all use the same written language. Chinese writing is not based on a phonetic alphabet. It is based on **ideograms**, pictures or characters that represent a thing or idea. To make the spoken language the same, most children are now taught the Mandarin dialect in school.

Chinese people follow several religions, especially Buddhism, Daoism, and Confucianism. Communist China discourages religion and encourages **atheism**, a denial that God exists.

> ### THE **BIG** IDEA
>
> **China has more people than any other country. Most share a common culture.**

■ GRAPHIC SUMMARY: *Population of China*

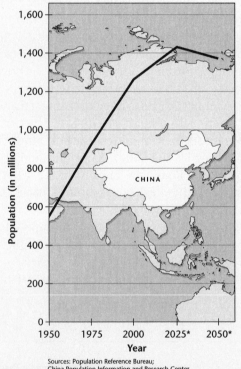

China's population has more than doubled since 1950.

Sources: Population Reference Bureau;
China Population Information and Research Center
*Projected population.

■ REVIEW QUESTIONS

1. How did Deng's Communist government control population growth?

2. **Graph Skills** Around what year did China's population reach 1 billion?

SECTION 4 CHINA'S NEIGHBORS

■ TEXT SUMMARY

Taiwan is an island off China's southeast coast. When the Chinese Nationalists were defeated in 1949, they fled to Taiwan, setting up a temporary **provisional government** there.

The Nationalists claimed to represent all of China. So did the mainland Communists. For many years, Western countries supported Taiwan. But in 1971, the United Nations recognized mainland China and removed Taiwan.

Most countries do not officially recognize Taiwan, but they trade with it. It has become one of Asia's leading economic powers.

The Nationalists improved Taiwan's farming and industry. The standard of living is high, and the people have maintained their culture. Until 1987, people in Taiwan had no official contact with China. Now they are investing money in China's Special Economic Zones.

Hong Kong is located on China's southern coast. Beginning in 1898, the British had a 99-year lease on Hong Kong. During that time Hong Kong became a leader in world trade. In 1997, Britain returned it to China. China agreed to allow economic and political freedom.

Mongolia is a vast, dry land. The Gobi Desert occupies the south. The rest has mostly steppe vegetation. In the 1200s, Genghiz Khan ruled a huge Mongol empire. Later Mongolia came under Chinese rule.

In 1911, Mongolia declared its independence. Ten years later, Mongolia became a communist country. Mongolia held democratic elections after Russia ended its communist system in the early 1990s.

> ### THE **BIG** IDEA
>
> **Taiwan is a leading economic power in Asia. Mongolia is gradually becoming more modern and democratic. The British returned Hong Kong to China in 1997.**

■ GRAPHIC SUMMARY: *China and its Neighbors*

Country	Population	Life Expectancy (years)	Per Capita GDP (in US $)
China	1,236,914,658	69.6	740
Mongolia	2,578,530	61.5	340
Taiwan	22,256,000	75.0	NA

Sources: *Microsoft Encarta Interactive World Atlas 2000* and Population Reference Bureau

NA indicates data not available.

The countries in East Asia differ from one another in many ways.

■ REVIEW QUESTIONS

1. Which country represented China in the United Nations in the 1950s?

2. Chart Skills Which country has the longest life expectancy?

CHAPTER 31 *Test*

◼ IDENTIFYING MAIN IDEAS

Write the letter of the correct answer in the blank provided. (10 points each)

____ **1.** What was the Long March?
   A. the Communists' journey to the mountains of China
   B. the Nationalists' escape to Taiwan
   C. the emperor's escape after he abdicated
   D. another name for the Great Leap Forward

____ **2.** Why did Nationalists and Communists cooperate during World War II?
   A. They thought a democratic election would end their fighting.
   B. They both wanted farmers to move to collective farms.
   C. They both wanted to drive out the Japanese who invaded China.
   D. The emperor forced them to cooperate.

____ **3.** What do the Special Economic Zones do?
   A. improve farm production
   B. attract foreign money in China
   C. destroy old ideas
   D. bring industry to the Gobi Desert

____ **4.** Which is NOT true about the Huang He?
   A. It is a transportation route.
   B. Floods caused many people to die.
   C. People caused Huang He's floods.
   D. People caused the Huang He to run dry.

____ **5.** The Plateau of Tibet is located in China's
   A. Northeast
   B. Southeast
   C. Northwest
   D. Southwest

____ **6.** After Chinese invaded Tibet, they
   A. rebuilt many Buddhist monasteries.
   B. destroyed many Buddhist monasteries.
   C. invited the Dalai Lama to return.
   D. brought in many other religions.

____ **7.** Deng Xiaoping tried to reduce China's population growth by telling each family to have
   A. no children.
   B. no more than one child.
   C. no more than two children.
   D. no more than three children.

____ **8.** One thing that the people of China share is
   A. a system of writing.
   B. a spoken language.
   C. a belief in Christianity.
   D. a belief in atheism.

____ **9.** How do most other countries today treat Taiwan?
   A. They do not recognize Taiwan, but they trade with it.
   B. They recognize Taiwan, but they do not trade with it.
   C. They neither recognize nor trade with Taiwan.
   D. They recognize Taiwan as the true government of China.

____ **10.** Why is Hong Kong now part of China?
   A. The people of Hong Kong voted to be part of China.
   B. The people of China voted for Hong Kong to be part of China.
   C. Britain returned Hong Kong to China at the end of a 99-year lease.
   D. Hong Kong's economy was failing, and Britain no longer wanted it.

Japan and the Koreas

SECTION 1 — JAPAN: THE LAND OF THE RISING SUN

TEXT SUMMARY

Japan calls itself the Land of the Rising Sun because ancient Japanese thought it was the first land to see the rising sun.

Japan is a chain of islands off the coast of East Asia. Most people live on four large islands, especially Honshu, the largest island. Only some land is good for farming. To create more farmland, people built terraces into hillsides and drained swamps.

Japan is part of the Ring of Fire, an area with many earthquakes and active volcanoes. **Seismographs**, machines that register movements in the earth's crust, are used to record the thousands of earthquakes that strike Japan each year. The climate varies with latitude. The northern island of Hokkaido has long winters and cool summers. Southern Honshu has hot summers and mild winters. Monsoons affect Japan and vary by season. **Typhoons** occur from late summer to early fall. They are tropical hurricanes that cause floods and landslides.

Japan is one of the most densely populated countries. Although Japan is about the same size as California, it has nearly four times that state's population. In crowded cities, prices for land and housing are high. To solve problems of pollution and waste disposal, Japan recycles 50 percent of its solid waste.

More than 99 percent of Japan's people share a common heritage and language. They also share a religion, Shinto. Shintoists worship forces of nature and their ancestors' spirits. Most Japanese also practice Buddhism. As Japan grew more modern, its middle class grew. Today, most Japanese are middle class.

THE BIG IDEA

Japan is made up of islands. The people belong to the same ethnic group and share a common culture.

GRAPHIC SUMMARY:
Japan and the Koreas

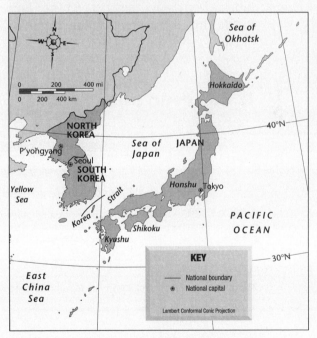

Japan and the Koreas have coasts on the Sea of Japan.

REVIEW QUESTIONS

1. What do Japanese people share that gives them unity?

2. **Map Skills** List Japan's four big islands from south to north.

JAPAN'S ECONOMIC DEVELOPMENT

▨ TEXT SUMMARY

THE **BIG** IDEA

Japan developed from an isolated agricultural country to a modern industrial power. Despite its lack of natural resources, its economy grew quickly.

When Japan had its first contact with the West, it was a wealthy and highly developed civilization. It welcomed Portuguese visitors in 1543. Later, Japan worried that European nations would try to conquer it. In 1639, it ordered Europeans to leave and closed its doors to the West.

Beginning in 1853, Western nations forced Japan to sign unequal treaties. In 1868, the new Meiji government began to make Japan more modern and industrial. By 1900, it ended the unequal treaties with the West.

Japan has few natural resources. It fought to take control of weaker nations that had resources. In the early 1900s, Japan won wars against China and Russia. In 1910, it made Korea part of Japan.

The worldwide depression that began in 1929 ruined Japanese businesses. Military leaders wanted an overseas empire to gain markets and raw materials. Japan became a military dictatorship. The new leaders promoted **militarism**, the glorification of the military and a readiness for war.

Japan sided with Nazi Germany during World War II. It attacked the United States naval base at Pearl Harbor, Hawaii, in 1941. In August 1945, Japan surrendered, after the United States dropped atomic bombs on two Japanese cities.

United States troops occupied Japan until 1952. They began democratic reforms. Japan was not allowed to rebuild its military.

After World War II, Japan had the world's fastest-growing economy. It imported raw materials and exported finished goods. One reason for Japan's success is its educated work force.

▨ GRAPHIC SUMMARY: *Japan's Economic Success*

REASONS FOR JAPAN'S ECONOMIC SUCCESS
• People are very highly educated.
• Companies encourage loyalty and team spirit.
• Japan is located at the center of trade routes.
• The government takes an active role in business.

There are a variety of reasons why Japan has been economically successful.

▨ REVIEW QUESTIONS

1. Since World War II, how has Japan dealt with a lack of natural resources?

2. **Chart Skills** Why has Japan been economically successful?

THE KOREAS: A DIVIDED PENINSULA

◼ TEXT SUMMARY

North Korea is a Communist country. South Korea is not. But both countries' people share a common history and culture.

After World War II, the Soviet Union took charge of North Korea and set up a Communist government. The United States supervised southern Korea. Elections were held in South Korea, and United States troops left in 1949.

In 1950, North Korea attacked South Korea to unite the country under communism. United Nations forces, including United States troops, helped South Korea. In 1953, a cease-fire ended the war. A **demilitarized zone**—an area with no troops or weapons allowed—separates the two Koreas.

North Korea has rich natural resources and its rivers have been harnessed for electric power.

South Korea has more than twice as many people and is densely populated. Almost a quarter of its people live in Seoul, the capital. Its flatter land and warmer climate make it more suitable for agriculture than North Korea.

Communist countries traded with North Korea. South Korea traded with the United States and Japan. South Korea built industries and nuclear power plants. As its economy grew, so did the middle class. South Korea's economy and standard of living are stronger than that of its neighbor.

Many Koreans want the two parts to unite, but North Korea wants communism while South Korea does not. In the late 1990s, North Korea suffered flooding, famine, and economic disaster.

THE **BIG** IDEA

The Korean Peninsula has been divided since 1945 into two countries: North Korea and South Korea. People in both countries share a common language and culture. South Korea's capitalist system has boomed, but North Korea's Communist economy has suffered.

◼ GRAPHIC SUMMARY: *Facts about Japan and the Two Koreas*

Country	Population	Life Expectancy (years)	Per Capita GDP (in US $)
Japan	125,931,533	80.0	33,230
North Korea	21,234,387	51.3	NA
South Korea	46,416,796	74.0	9,620

Source: *Microsoft Encarta Interactive World Atlas 2000*
NA indicates data not available.

South Korea is slightly smaller in area than North Korea, but their populations are very different in size.

◼ REVIEW QUESTIONS

1. What caused Korea to separate into two countries?

2. Chart Skills Which of the Koreas has a larger population?

CHAPTER 32 *Test*

◨ IDENTIFYING MAIN IDEAS

Write the letter of the correct answer in the blank provided. (10 points each)

_____ 1. On which island do most Japanese live?
  A. Hokkaido
  B. Kyushu
  C. Shikoku
  D. Honshu

_____ 2. What are typhoons?
  A. weather patterns that occur year-round in Japan
  B. tropical hurricanes
  C. the Japanese word for monsoons
  D. the Japanese word for population

_____ 3. What is Shinto?
  A. a religion shared by most Japanese
  B. a religion the Japanese outlawed
  C. a densely populated area in Japan
  D. a Japanese political party

_____ 4. What has happened to Japan's middle class since World War II?
  A. It nearly disappeared.
  B. It remained about the same size.
  C. It grew a little.
  D. It grew to include the majority of Japanese.

_____ 5. Why did Japan order foreigners to leave in 1639?
  A. The foreigners were too backward in industry.
  B. Japan worried that foreigners wanted its rich natural resources.
  C. Japan feared foreigners would try to conquer it.
  D. The foreigners were taking all the good farmland.

_____ 6. What changes did the Meiji government make?
  A. It started making Japan more modern and industrial.
  B. It brought Buddhism to Japan.
  C. It became very warlike.
  D. It gave Japanese women the right to vote.

_____ 7. What happened to Japan's military after World War II?
  A. The military began rebuilding its weapons.
  B. The military started a new war.
  C. The military was not allowed to rebuild.
  D. All the military leaders were executed.

_____ 8. When did Korea become two separate countries?
  A. after Japan invaded in 1910
  B. after World War I
  C. after World War II
  D. in the 1980s

_____ 9. What is a demilitarized zone?
  A. a strip of land where troops and weapons are not allowed
  B. an area where military leaders aim guns at one another
  C. a country that is at peace with its neighbors
  D. a war zone

_____ 10. What prevents North Korea and South Korea from reuniting?
  A. Their people do not speak the same language.
  B. The Korean people do not want them to reunite.
  C. The United Nations will not let them reunite.
  D. They cannot agree on the form of government a united Korea would have.

Southeast Asia

SECTION 1 · *HISTORICAL INFLUENCES ON SOUTHEAST ASIA*

TEXT SUMMARY

Southeast Asia's location makes it one of the world's great geographic crossroads. Many came to trade, leaving behind many cultures. The earliest settlers of the mainland probably came from China and South Asia. Later, people came from central Asia. No group ever united the region, but several powerful kingdoms arose.

Traders and priests came from India and brought Hinduism and Buddhism. The people of Southeast Asia absorbed these religions into their existing religious beliefs. Muslim traders from Arabia and India brought Islam.

Many Chinese migrated to Southeast Asia. They controlled northern Vietnam for about 1,000 years, starting in 100 B.C. Chinese culture affected Vietnam's language, religion, art, government, and farming. But the Vietnamese never lost their identity.

Europeans came for silks, spices, and precious metals. By the late 1800s, the Europeans had colonized all of Southeast Asia except Thailand. Europeans greatly changed the region's physical and human geography. They cleared forests for plantations to grow coffee, tea, tobacco, and other cash crops. Many small Southeast Asian farmers had to work on plantations. Europeans also sold factory goods to their colonies, hurting local crafts.

Europeans built roads and railroads. These helped port cities grow and attracted people from China and India. Conflicts arose between new immigrants and **indigenous**, or native, Southeast Asians. When Europeans carved out colonies, different ethnic groups were combined in one colony, while members of the same group were divided. After independence, conflicts between ethnic groups remained.

> ### THE **BIG** IDEA
>
> **Over time, many different ethnic groups settled in Southeast Asia, influencing its culture and religion. European control affected its geography.**

GRAPHIC SUMMARY: *Southeast Asian Cultures*

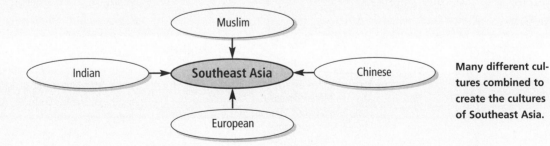

Many different cultures combined to create the cultures of Southeast Asia.

REVIEW QUESTIONS

1. What major religions are found in Southeast Asia?

2. **Diagram Skills** What were the four main influences on Southeast Asia's cultures?

THE COUNTRIES OF SOUTHEAST ASIA

▣ TEXT SUMMARY

Most countries in the region belong to the Association of Southeast Asian Nations (ASEAN). ASEAN promotes economic cooperation and peace among its members.

Unity within each country of Southeast Asia has been difficult to achieve. Myanmar, formerly called Burma, was a British colony until 1948. Since independence, several ethnic groups have fought against military dictatorship. Warfare and **insurgents**, people who rebel against their government, have slowed Myanmar's economic growth. Thailand, the only country in Southeast Asia that did not become a European colony, has a strong national identity and a successful economy.

Vietnam was a French colony. After World War II, France wanted it back. Ho Chi Minh declared Vietnam's independence and defeated the French in 1954. Vietnam was divided into Communist North Vietnam and non-Communist South Vietnam. War broke out when the Communists in the North and South tried to reunite the two countries. The United States entered the war to help South Vietnam.

South Vietnam fell to the Communists in 1975. Vietnam reunited one year later. In the 1990s, Vietnam attracted foreign investors, and its economy boomed.

Indonesia is made up of more than 13,000 islands. The people speak more than 250 languages and dialects. The Philippines were ruled by the Spanish, and then by the United States. It became independent in 1946. The Roman Catholic religion and Spanish culture unify ethnic groups.

The tiny island of Singapore is an economic power.

THE BIG IDEA

National unity is difficult for many of these countries because of ethnic differences. Although most of these nations had an economic boom, some have political dictatorships.

▣ GRAPHIC SUMMARY: *Similarities and Differences among Vietnam, Laos, and Cambodia*

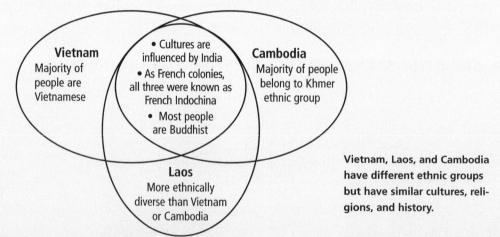

Vietnam Majority of people are Vietnamese

- Cultures are influenced by India
- As French colonies, all three were known as French Indochina
- Most people are Buddhist

Cambodia Majority of people belong to Khmer ethnic group

Laos More ethnically diverse than Vietnam or Cambodia

Vietnam, Laos, and Cambodia have different ethnic groups but have similar cultures, religions, and history.

▣ REVIEW QUESTIONS

1. How has Vietnam changed recently?

2. **Diagram Skills** What do Vietnam, Laos, and Cambodia have in common?

CHAPTER 33 *Test*

IDENTIFYING MAIN IDEAS

Write the letter of the correct answer in the blank provided. (10 points each)

____ 1. What are two major religions of Southeast Asia?
  A. Shinto and Hinduism
  B. Christianity and Hinduism
  C. Buddhism and Islam
  D. Daoism and Confucianism

____ 2. What country controlled northern Vietnam for about 1,000 years?
  A. India
  B. China
  C. Indonesia
  D. Malaysia

____ 3. What first drew European countries to Southeast Asia?
  A. oil and natural gas
  B. invitations from countries in the region
  C. a need for more railroads
  D. silks, spices, and precious metals

____ 4. What changes did Europeans make in Southeast Asia?
  A. They created plantations and built railroads.
  B. They changed the religion of most people in the region.
  C. They encouraged local crafts.
  D. They helped small farmers work their farms.

____ 5. What problems remained in Southeast Asia after countries became independent?
  A. They did not have enough plantations.
  B. The countries in the region had no leaders.
  C. They had no port cities.
  D. Ethnic groups fought with each other.

____ 6. What is ASEAN?
  A. a group of European countries that rule Southeast Asia
  B. an association that works for coopera-tion among countries in Southeast Asia
  C. a Communist government in Southeast Asia
  D. a form of money used in Southeast Asia

____ 7. Which Southeast Asian country remained independent during colonial times?
  A. Burma
  B. Vietnam
  C. Thailand
  D. Indonesia

____ 8. What led to the war in Vietnam?
  A. South Vietnam wanted a communist government and invaded North Vietnam.
  B. The French insisted that Vietnam be an independent country.
  C. The Communists in North and South Vietnam wanted to reunite the two countries under a communist government.
  D. North Vietnam wanted more invest-ments from the United States and Europe.

____ 9. Which country ruled the Philippines until 1946?
  A. Thailand
  B. the United States
  C. Britain
  D. France

____ 10. What tiny country is an important economic power?
  A. Singapore
  B. Indonesia
  C. Myanmar
  D. the Philippines

The Pacific World and Antarctica

SECTION 1 AUSTRALIA

■ TEXT SUMMARY

THE BIG IDEA

Australia has a small population because of its location and climate. Its major cities are near the coast. Ranching and mining are important activities in Australia.

Australia is both a country and a continent. It is the world's sixth largest country and the smallest continent. Scientists think that Australia's first people, called **Aborigines**, arrived more than 50,000 years ago, probably from Southeast Asia. They lived by hunting and gathering plants.

In 1770, Britain claimed the land. European settlement in Australia began in 1787 when British prisoners were sent from overcrowded British prisons. After their release, many prisoners stayed. Other British settlers came for land on which to raise sheep and grow wheat. Many Aborigines died from European diseases or weapons. Their number declined from 300,000 in the 1700s to only about 50,000 today. After World War II, immigrants came from Greece, Italy, and other parts of Europe. Today, many come from Southeast Asia, drawn by Australia's high standard of living.

Australia's harsh climate has greatly affected where people live. The interior is very hot and dry. Most people live along the eastern and southeastern coasts, where the climate is moist.

Most of Australia west of the Great Dividing Range is arid plain or dry plateau. This harsh wilderness region is known as the **outback**. The Aborigines were the first to live there. European settlers found gold and other minerals. Some built farms and huge ranches for sheep and cattle. Australian sheep supply meat and merino wool.

■ GRAPHIC SUMMARY:
Australia and New Zealand

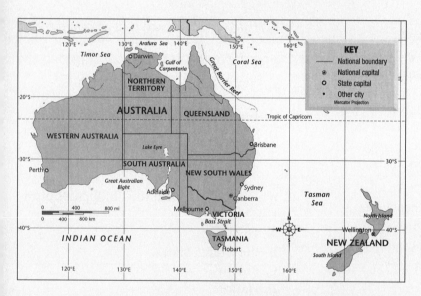

Australia is divided into seven states.

■ REVIEW QUESTIONS

1. According to scientists, who were the first Australians?

2. Map Skills What are Australia's seven state capitals?

NEW ZEALAND AND THE PACIFIC ISLANDS

■ TEXT SUMMARY

Many tiny islands dot the vast Pacific Ocean. Two of the larger islands, called North Island and South Island, make up the country of New Zealand. North Island is narrow and hilly, with a central plateau and active volcanoes. There are many **geysers**, hot springs that shoot out jets of steam and hot water into the air. South Island has New Zealand's highest mountains.

■ GRAPHIC SUMMARY:
Comparing Australia, New Zealand, and the Pacific Islands

Country	Population	Life Expectancy (years)	Per Capita GDP (in US $)
Australia	18,613,087	79.9	22,200
Fiji	802,611	66.33	7,300
Marshall Islands	63,031	64.5	1,670
New Zealand	3,625,388	77.5	17,400
Palau	18,110	67.5	8,800
Samoa	224,713	69.0	2,100
Solomon Islands	441,039	71.8	2,650
Vanuatu	185,204	61.0	1,300

Sources: *Microsoft Encarta Interactive World Atlas 2000* and *CIA World Factbook 2000*

The countries of this region vary greatly in size and GDP.

The Maori were the first people to live in New Zealand. Europeans arrived in 1769. In 1840, the Maori accepted British rule in exchange for land rights. Today, the Maori number less than 10 percent of the population.

New Zealand is an agricultural country with dairy cows and sheep. Yet a majority of people live in large cities along the coast.

Many Pacific islands, called high islands, are the tops of underwater mountains. Low islands, called **atolls**, can also be found in the Pacific. An atoll is a ring-shaped coral island surrounding a lagoon.

The Pacific Islands are divided into three groups: Melanesia, Micronesia, and Polynesia. Farming, fishing, and tourism are the islands' main economic activities. After World War II, the Pacific Islands were divided into **trust territories**, or territories supervised by other nations. Most Pacific islands became independent in the 1960s and 1970s.

THE BIG IDEA

Most New Zealanders are of European descent. The Maori are a minority. The two kinds of Pacific islands are high islands and low islands.

■ REVIEW QUESTIONS

1. Who are the Maori?

2. **Chart Skills** What Pacific country has the largest population after Australia and New Zealand?

ANTARCTICA

◼ TEXT SUMMARY

The continent of Antarctica is covered and surrounded by ice. Early exploration of this region was difficult. Now, forty countries share scientific research in Antarctica.

Antarctica is a frozen continent, with no permanent human settlers. Few plants and animals can survive in its icy conditions. Antarctica has many different kinds of ice. Scientists from many countries spend time doing research in Antarctica.

Antarctica was the last of the world's continents to be explored. It was first seen by sailors from Russia, Great Britain, and the United States. Humans did not set foot on the continent until 1895.

Some nations tried to claim parts of Antarctica, but claims were not recognized because no country had permanent settlers there. Antarctica's greatest resource is its wealth of scientific information. Scientists worked to convince the world that the continent should remain open to all countries that wanted to conduct research there. In 1961, twelve nations signed the Antarctic Treaty for peaceful use of the continent and sharing of scientific research. These nations and twenty-eight others renewed the treaty in 1989.

◼ GRAPHIC SUMMARY: *The Antarctic Treaty*

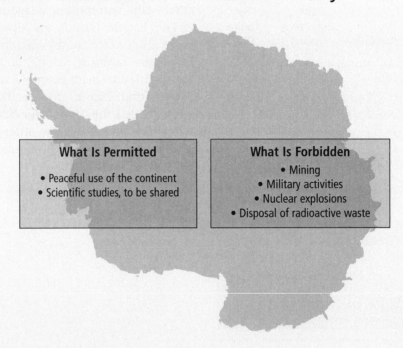

What Is Permitted
- Peaceful use of the continent
- Scientific studies, to be shared

What Is Forbidden
- Mining
- Military activities
- Nuclear explosions
- Disposal of radioactive waste

Forty countries have agreed to honor the Antarctic Treaty.

◼ REVIEW QUESTIONS

1. Why did countries refuse to recognize claims to Antarctica?

2. **Chart Skills** What activities are forbidden under the Antarctic Treaty?

CHAPTER 34 *Test*

■ IDENTIFYING MAIN IDEAS

Write the letter of the correct answer in the blank provided. (10 points each)

____ **1.** The Aborigines were the first people to settle in
  A. Malaysia.
  B. Indonesia.
  C. New Zealand.
  D. Australia.

____ **2.** The first large group of British settlers in Australia came as
  A. explorers.
  B. sheep herders.
  C. prisoners.
  D. explorers.

____ **3.** What is Australia's outback?
  A. the arid area that covers much of Australia's interior
  B. Australia's coastal areas with many cities
  C. the prisons where British convicts were sent
  D. the highest mountains on the continent

____ **4.** What is a geyser?
  A. a fruit grown in New Zealand
  B. a mountain ridge
  C. a volcanic mountain
  D. a hot spring that shoots out steam and hot water

____ **5.** Who were the first settlers in New Zealand?
  A. the British
  B. the Dutch
  C. the Maori
  D. the Aborigines

____ **6.** Atolls are
  A. tops of underwater mountains.
  B. ring-shaped islands.
  C. islands that people created by bringing in soil.
  D. colonies of other countries.

____ **7.** What is a trust territory?
  A. a country that is supervised by another country
  B. a country that supervises another country
  C. a country that wants to become a state of a larger country
  D. a permanent colony

____ **8.** What countries own Antarctica?
  A. Russia and the United States
  B. Great Britain and France
  C. the United States and Great Britain
  D. None; it is a research center for many countries.

____ **9.** Antarctica's greatest resource is
  A. its variety of plants and flowers.
  B. its many kinds of ice.
  C. its diverse ethnic background.
  D. its wealth of scientific information.

____ **10.** The Antarctic Treaty
  A. grants ownership of the continent to several countries.
  B. allows all countries to make peaceful use of the continent.
  C. allows military activity and nuclear explosions.
  D. is limited to only a few countries.

GLOSSARY

A

abdicate to surrender one's office, throne, or authority (pp. 71, 108)

Aborigine an original inhabitant; one of the original inhabitants of Australia (p. 120)

absolute location the position on the earth in which a place can be found (p. 5)

agricultural revolution the change from nomadic hunting and gathering to farming that took place about 8000 B.C. (p. 74)

anarchy political disorder and violence; lawlessness (p. 81)

annex to formally incorporate into a country or state the territory of another (p. 68)

apartheid formerly in the Republic of South Africa, the policy of strict racial segregation (p. 97)

aqueduct a large pipe or channel designed to transport water from a remote source over a long distance (p. 26)

archipelago a group of islands (p. 38)

atheism the belief that God does not exist (p. 110)

atoll a ring-shaped coral island surrounding a lagoon (p. 121)

authoritarian descriptive of a system of government in which the leaders hold all political power (p. 13)

autonomous region a political unit with limited self-government (p. 109)

autonomy independence (p. 76)

ayatollah a religious leader among Shiite Muslims (p. 83)

B

balkanize to break up into small, mutually hostile political units, as occurred in the Balkans after World War I (p. 67)

bauxite a mineral used in making aluminum (p. 43)

biome the term used to describe a major type of ecosystem that can be found in various regions throughout the world (p. 10)

black market the system of selling goods and services outside of official channels (p. 72)

blight a plant disease (p. 51)

bog an area of wet, spongy ground (p. 50)

boycott to refuse to purchase or use a product or service as an expression of disapproval (p. 102)

C

canton a political division or state; one of the states in Switzerland (p. 57)

caravan a large group of merchants who join together to travel in safety (p. 88)

cash crop a farm crop grown for sale and profit (p. 35)

caste system a social hierarchy in which a person possesses a distinct rank in society that is determined by birth (p. 103)

chaparral a type of natural vegetation that is adapted to Mediterranean climates; small evergreen trees and low bushes, or scrub (pp. 10, 74)

chemical weathering the process by which the actual chemical structure of rock is changed, usually when water and carbon dioxide cause a breakdown of the rock (p. 7)

chernozem a rich topsoil found in the Russian steppes and other mid-latitude grasslands (pp. 70, 77)

climate the term used for the weather patterns that an area typically experiences over a long period of time (p. 9)

collective farm a government-owned farm managed by workers who share the profits from their produce (p. 66)

colony a territory separated from but subject to a ruling power (p. 18)

command economy an economic system that is controlled by the central government (pp. 13, 32, 71)

commercial farming the raising of crops and livestock for sale in outside markets (p. 16)

communism a system of government in which the government controls the means of production, determining what goods will be made, how much workers will be paid, and how much items will cost (p. 63)

compulsory required (p. 47)

confederation a system of government in which individual political units keep their sovereignty but give limited power to a central government (p. 13)

coniferous cone-bearing; a type of tree able to survive long, cold winters, with long, thin needles rather than leaves (p. 10)

continent any of the seven large landmasses of the earth's surface: Africa, Antarctica, Asia, Australia, Europe, North America, and South America (p. 6)

continental divide a boundary or area of high ground that separates rivers flowing toward opposite sides of a continent (p. 18)

coral island an island formed by the skeletal remains of tiny sea animals and the sand and sediment piling on top of them (p. 38)

core the earth's center, consisting of very hot metal that is dense and solid in the inner core and molten, or liquid, in the outer core (p. 6)

cottage industry a small-scale manufacturing operation using little technology, often located in or near people's homes (p. 103)

coup the sudden overthrow of a ruler or government, often involving violent force or the threat of force (p. 91)

crust the solid, rocky, surface layer of the earth (p. 6)

cultural convergence the contact and interaction of one culture with another (p. 12)

cultural diffusion the process by which people adopt the practices of their neighbors (p. 47)

cultural divergence the restriction of a culture from outside influences (pp. 12, 51)

culture the way of life that distinguishes a people, for example, government, language, religion, customs, and beliefs (p. 12)

customs taxes or fees that a government charges on goods brought in from another country (p. 30)

czar an emperor of Russia (p. 71)

D

decentralize to transfer government power to smaller regions (p. 56)

deciduous leaf-shedding; a type of tree that sheds its leaves during one season (p. 10)

deforestation the process of stripping the land of its trees (pp. 41, 90)

demilitarized zone a strip of land on which troops or weapons are not allowed (p. 115)

democracy a system of government in which the people are invested with the power to choose their leaders and determine government policy (p. 13)

desalination the process of removing salt from seawater so that it can be used for drinking and irrigation (pp. 74, 82)

desertification the transformation of arable land into desert either naturally or through human intervention (pp. 77, 90)

dictatorship a system of government in which absolute power is held by a small group or one person (p. 13)

dike an embankment of earth and rock built to hold back water (p. 56)

diversify to increase the variety of (p. 68)

drip irrigation a process by which precisely controlled amounts of water drip directly onto plants from pipes, thus preserving precious water resources in dry areas (p. 80)

E

ecosystem the interaction of plant life, animal life, and the physical environment in which they live (p. 10)

embargo a severe restriction of trade with other countries (p. 81)

enclave a country completely surrounded by another country (p. 98)

entrepreneur a go-getter individual who starts and builds a business (p. 67)

erosion the movement of weathered materials, including gravel, soil, and sand, usually caused by water, wind, and glaciers (p. 7)

escarpment a steep cliff that separates two level areas of differing elevations (pp. 40, 85)

estuary the wide mouth of a river, where freshwater river currents meet salt water (p. 45)

ethnocracy a system of government in which one ethnic group rules over others (p. 96)

euro the common currency used by member nations of the European Union (p. 47)

export an item that is sent out of the country for sale (p. 16)

F

favela a slum community in a Brazilian city (p. 40)

federation a government structure in which the national government shares power with state or local governments (p. 13)

fertile able to produce abundantly (p. 49)

fjord a narrow valley or inlet from the sea, originally carved out by an advancing glacier and filled by melting glacial ice (p. 52)

fossil fuel any one of several nonrenewable mineral resources formed from the remains of ancient plants and animals and used for fuel (p. 15)

free enterprise an economic system that allows individuals to own, operate, and profit from their own businesses in an open, competitive market (p. 20)

fundamentalism a set of religious beliefs based on a strict interpretation of a sacred text (p. 77)

G

gasohol a fuel mixture of gasoline and ethanol (p. 41)

gaucho a cowboy who herded cattle in the pampas of Argentina and Uruguay (p. 45)

genocide the systematic killing or intentional destruction of a people (p. 76)

geography the study of the earth's surface and the processes that shape it, the connections between places, and the complex relationships between people and their environments (p. 5)

geothermal energy energy produced from the earth's intense interior heat (pp. 15, 52)

geyser a natural hot spring that shoots a column of water and steam into the air (p. 121)

ghetto a section of a city in which a particular minority group is forced to live (p. 65)

glacier a huge, slow-moving mass of snow and ice (p. 7)

glasnost a policy of openness introduced in the Soviet Union in the late 1980s (p. 71)

grain exchange a place where grain is bought and sold as a commodity (p. 25)

gross national product (GNP) the total value of a nation's goods and services, including the output of domestic firms in foreign countries and excluding the domestic output of foreign firms (p. 20)

growing season in farming, the average number of days between the last frost of spring and the first frost of fall (p. 25)

guerrilla a member of an armed force that is not part of a regular army; relating to a form of warfare carried on by such an independent armed force (p. 37)

H

harambee a policy of cooperation adopted in Kenya after independence to encourage economic growth (p. 95)

hierarchy rank according to function (p. 21)

Holocaust the execution of 6 million Jews in Nazi concentration camps during World War II (p. 65)

hurricane a destructive tropical storm that forms over the Atlantic Ocean, usually in late summer and early fall, with winds of at least 74 miles (119 km) per hour (p. 32)

hydroelectric power electricity that is generated by moving water (p. 104)

I

ideogram in written language, a character or symbol that represents an idea or thing (p. 110)

import an item that is brought into the country for sale (p. 16)

indigenous native to or living naturally in an area or environment (p. 117)

Industrial Revolution the shift from human power to machine power (p. 47)

inflation a sharp, widespread rise in prices (p. 55)

infrastructure the basic support facilities of a country, such as roads and bridges, power plants, and schools (p. 82)

inhabitable able to support permanent residents (p. 61)

insurgent a person who rebels against his or her government (p. 118)

intensive farming farming that requires a great deal of labor (p. 106)

International Monetary Fund (IMF) an agency of the United Nations that provides loans to countries for development projects (p. 92)

irrigation the watering of farmland with water drawn from reservoirs or rivers (pp. 34, 104)

isthmus a narrow strip of land having water on each side and joining two larger bodies of land (p. 37)

L

land redistribution a policy by which land is taken from those who own large amounts and redistributed to those who have little or none (p. 35)

leeward facing away from the wind (p. 38)

literacy the ability to read and write (pp. 18, 134)

llano a grassy plain (p. 43)

M

malnutrition disease caused by a lack of food or an unbalanced diet (p. 95)

mandate a commission from the League of Nations authorizing a nation to govern a territory (p. 79)

mantle a thick layer of mostly solid rock beneath the earth's crust that surrounds the earth's core (p. 6)

maritime bordering on or near the sea; relating to navigation or shipping (p. 28)

market economy an economic system in which decisions about production, price, and other economic factors are determined by the law of supply and demand (pp. 13, 32)

mechanical weathering the actual breaking up or physical weakening of rock by forces such as ice and roots (p. 7)

megalopolis a very large city; a region made up of several large cities and their surrounding areas, considered to be a single urban complex (p. 23)

mercenary a professional soldier hired by a foreign country (p. 93)

mestizo a person of mixed European and Native American heritage (p. 32)

metropolitan area a major city and its surrounding suburbs (p. 21)

migrant worker a worker who travels from place to place, working where extra help is needed to cultivate or harvest crops (p. 35)

militarism the glorification of the military and a readiness for war (p. 114)

mixed economy a system combining different degrees of government regulation (p. 52)

monarchy a system of authoritarian government headed by a monarch—a king, queen, shah, or sultan—whose position is usually inherited (p. 13)

monotheism the belief in one God (p. 74)

monsoon a seasonal shift in the prevailing winds that influences large climate regions (p. 100)

moor broad, treeless, rolling land, often poorly drained and having patches of marsh and peat bog (p. 50)

mulatto a person of mixed African and other ancestry (p. 43)

multiethnic composed of many ethnic groups (p. 63)

N

national identity a people's sense of what makes them a nation (p. 65)

nationalism pride in one's nation; the desire of a cultural group to rule themselves as a separate nation (pp. 76, 102)

natural resource a material in the natural environment that people value and use to satisfy their needs (p. 15)

navigable deep or wide enough to allow the passage of ships (p. 59)

nomadic herding the practice of moving flocks to different pastures throughout the year (p. 85)

nonrenewable resource a natural resource that cannot be replaced once it is used (p. 15)

nonviolent resistance the policy of opposing an enemy or oppressor by any means other than violence (p. 102)

nuclear energy a type of energy produced by fission—the splitting of uranium atoms in a nuclear reactor, releasing stored energy (p. 15)

O

ore a rocky material containing a valuable mineral (p. 49)

outback remote, sparsely settled, arid, rural country, especially the central and western plains and plateaus of Australia (p. 120)

P

pampas a grasslands region in Argentina and Uruguay (pp. 32, 45)

partition a division into separate parts (p. 102)

peat spongy material containing waterlogged and decaying mosses and plants, sometimes dried and used as fuel (p. 51)

peninsula a strip of land that juts out into an ocean (p. 34)

perestroika in the former Soviet Union, a policy of economic restructuring (p. 71)

permafrost a layer of soil just below the earth's surface that stays permanently frozen (p. 70)

piedmont a region of rolling foothills (p. 45)

plateau an area of high, flat land (p. 85)

plate tectonics the theory that the earth's outer shell is composed of a number of large, unanchored plates, or slabs of rock, whose constant movement explains earthquakes and volcanic activity (p. 6)

poaching illegal hunting (p. 74)

polder an area of low-lying land that has been reclaimed from the sea (p. 56)

population density the average number of people living in a given area (p. 12)

precipitation all the forms of water that fall to earth from the atmosphere, including rain and snow (p. 9)

prevailing westerlies the constant flow of air from west to east in the temperate zones of the earth (p. 47)

primary economic activity an economic activity that takes or uses natural resources directly, such as fishing or mining (p. 16)

privatization the process of selling government-owned industries and businesses to private owners (p. 66)

province a territory governed as a political division of a country (p. 28)

provisional government a temporary government pending permanent arrangements (p. 111)

Q

quaternary economic activity an economic activity that focuses on the acquisition, processing, and sharing of information, such as education or research (p. 16)

R

recession an extended decline in business activity (p. 54)

refugee a person who flees his or her country to escape danger or unfair treatment (p. 90)

relative location the position of a place in relation to another place (p. 5)

Renaissance the revival of art, literature, and learning that took place in Europe during the fourteenth, fifteenth, and sixteenth centuries (p. 60)

renewable resource a natural resource that the environment continues to supply or replace as it is used (p. 15)

reparation money paid for war damages (p. 55)

reservoir a natural or artificial lake used to collect water for human needs (p. 87)

revolution one complete orbit of the earth around the sun. The earth completes one revolution every 365¼ days, or one year (p. 9)

S

Sahel the region in Africa just south of the Sahara (p. 85)

sanction an action taken by the international community to punish a country for unacceptable behaviors (p. 97)

savanna a tropical grassland with scattered trees, located in the warm lands nearest the Equator (p. 10)

secede to withdraw formally from membership in a political or religious organization (p. 29)

secondary economic activity an economic activity in which people use raw materials to produce or manufacture new products of greater value (p. 16)

segregation the separation of the races (p. 97)

seismograph an instrument that measures and records movement in the earth's crust (p. 113)

self-determination the right of a people to decide their own political future (p. 79)

selva a forested region in Ecuador, Peru, and Bolivia (p. 44)

separatism a movement to win political, religious, or ethnic independence from another group (p. 29)

sertão a region in Brazil with poor soil and uncertain rain (p. 40)

shah the title of the former ruler of Iran (p. 83)

shifting agriculture the practice of farming a site until the soil is exhausted, then moving on to a new site (p. 90)

sirocco a hot, dry wind from northern Africa (p. 59)

solar energy energy produced by the sun (p. 15)

sovereignty a country's freedom and power to decide on policies and actions (p. 13)

sphere of influence an area or country that is politically and economically dominated by, though not directly governed by, another country (p. 108)

standard of living a person's or group's level of material well-being, as measured by education, housing, health care, and nutrition (p. 18)

steppe (step) a temperate grassland found in Europe and Asia (p. 63)

subcontinent a large landmass forming a distinct part of a continent (p. 100)

subsistence economy See *traditional economy*

subsistence farming farming that provides only enough for the needs of a family or a village (p. 16)

summit the highest point of a mountain or similar elevation (p. 47)

Sunbelt the southern and southwestern states of the United States, from the Carolinas to southern California, characterized by a warm climate and, recently, rapid population growth (p. 24)

T

taiga thinly scattered, coniferous forests found in Europe and Asia (p. 63)

telecommunications communication by electronic means (p. 20)

terrace in farming, a flat, narrow ledge of land, usually constructed in hilly areas to increase the amount of arable land (p. 106)

tertiary economic activity an economic activity in which people do not directly gather or process raw materials but pursue activities that serve others; service industry (p. 16)

theocrat someone who claims to rule by religious or divine authority (p. 109)

traditional economy an economic system in which families produce goods and services for their own use, with little surplus and exchange of goods; also known as a subsistence economy (pp. 13, 32)

tropical storm a storm with winds of at least 39 miles per hour (p. 32)

trust territory a dependent colony or territory supervised by another country by commission of the United Nations (p. 121)

tundra a region where temperatures are always cool or cold and only specialized plants can grow (pp. 10, 26, 63, 70)

typhoon a destructive tropical storm that forms over the Pacific Ocean (p. 113)

U

unitary system a system of government in which one central government holds most of the political power (p. 13)

urbanization the growth of city populations (p. 12)

V

villagization a political movement by which rural people are forced to move to towns and work on collective farms (p. 96)

W

weather the condition of the bottom layer of the earth's atmosphere in one place over a short period of time (p. 9)

weathering the chemical or mechanical process by which rock is gradually broken down, eventually becoming soil (p. 7)

windward facing the wind (p. 38)

World Bank an agency of the United Nations that provides loans to countries for development projects (p. 92)

Z

Zionist a member of a movement known as Zionism, founded to promote the establishment of an independent Jewish state (p. 79)

INDEX

A

Aborigines, 120
Afghanistan, 104
Africa, 59, 79, 85, 87–88, 90–93, 95–98
Afrikaners, 97
agricultural revolution, 74
agriculture. *See* farming.
Alabama, 24
Alaska, 26
Albania, 67
Alberta, Canada, 28
Algeria, 88
Alps, 47, 54, 57, 60
Amazon rain forest, 32, 41
Amazon River, 40
Amu Darya River, 77
Andes, 44–45
Angola, 98
Antarctic Treaty, 122
Antarctica, 122
apartheid, 97
Apennine Mountains, 60
aqueduct, 26
Arab-Israeli wars, 81
Arabian Peninsula, 82
Arabs, 79–80, 85, 87–88
Aral Sea, 77
Arctic Ocean, 70
Argentina, 45
Armenia, 76
Asia, 18, 29, 59, 70, 74, 77, 79–81, 85, 88, 100, 102–104, 106, 111, 113, 117–118, 120
Association of Southeast Asian Nations (ASEAN), 118
Aswan High Dam, 87
Atacama Desert, 44
Atatürk, 83
atheism, 110
Athens, Greece, 61
Atlanta, Georgia, 24
Atlantic Ocean, 21, 23, 28, 30, 43, 45
atoll, 121
atomic bomb, 114
Australia, 106, 120
Austria, 57
Austro-Hungarian Empire, 57
ayatollah, 83
Azerbaijan, 76
Aztecs, 32, 35

B

Bahamas, 38
Bahrain, 82
Baja California peninsula, 34
Balkan Peninsula, 67
Baltic Sea, 68
Baluchistan Plateau, 104
Bangladesh, 102, 104
Barcelona, Spain, 59

Basques, 59
bauxite, 43, 45
Beijing, China, 108, 109
Belarus, 68
Belgium, 56
Benelux countries, 56
Berlin Wall, 55
Bhutan, 100, 104
Bilbao, Spain, 59
biome, 10
Black Sea, 67, 74, 76
Boers, 97
bogs, 50
Bolivia, 44–45
Bordeaux, France, 54
Bosnia-Herzegovina, 67
Boston, Massachusetts, 23
Botswana, 98
boycott, 102
Brasília, Brazil, 40–41
Brazil, 40–41, 45
Brazzaville, Congo Republic, 93
Britain, 29, 87, 102, 111, 120. *See also* England, Great Britain.
British Columbia, Canada, 28
Buddhism, 100, 110, 113, 117
Buddhists, 109
Bulgaria, 67
Burkina Faso, 90
Burma. *See* Myanmar.
Burundi, 96
Byzantine Empire, 61

C

Canada, 18, 28–30, 56
Canadian Shield, 28
canton, 57
capitalism, 63
caravans, 88
Caribbean islands, 32, 38
Caribbean Sea, 32, 38, 44
cash crop, 35, 95
Caspian Sea, 74, 76–77
caste system, 103
Catholics, 51, 60, 65
Caucasus Mountains, 76
Caucasus nations, 76
Celtic tribes, 51
Central African Republic, 93
Central America, 37
Central Asia, 74
Chad, 90, 93
Chechnya, 72
Chernobyl, 68
chernozem, 70, 77
Chicago, Illinois, 21
Chile, 44
China, 77, 106, 108–111, 114, 117. *See also* People's Republic of China.
Christianity, 60, 63, 71, 74, 76, 81, 96

Church of England, 50
cities, 21, 23–26, 30, 40–41, 44–45, 57, 60, 71, 74, 77, 81, 87–88, 90, 100, 103, 113, 117, 121
climate, 9, 18, 24–26, 28, 32, 34, 38, 43–44, 47, 51–52, 59, 63, 70–71, 76–77, 85, 90–92, 95, 100, 106, 113, 115, 120
coal, 15, 20, 25, 49–50, 54–55, 68, 76, 98
coffee, 40, 43, 117
collective farm, 66, 68, 96, 108
Colombia, 43
colony, 18, 35, 59, 85, 117–118
command economy, 13, 32, 71–72
Commonwealth of Nations, 30
communications, 20, 82
communism, 55, 63, 65–68, 71, 76, 98, 108, 110–111, 115, 118
confederation, 13, 57
Confucianism, 110
Congo Basin, 93
Congo Republic, 93
Congo River, 93
continent, 6, 18, 37, 45, 63, 100, 120, 122
continental divide, 18
core, earth's, 6
cottage industry, 103
coup, 91–92
Crete, 61
Croatia, 67
crust, earth's, 6
Cuba, 38
Cultural Revolution, 108
culture, 12, 29–30, 43, 47, 51, 61, 76, 83, 85, 92, 100, 106, 109–111, 115, 117
customs, 30
Cyprus, 83
czar, 71
Czech Republic, 66
Czechoslovakia, 66

D

Dalai Lama, 109
Dallas, Texas, 24
Danube River, 66
Daoism, 110
de Klerk, F.W., 97
Dead Sea, 80
deforestation, 41, 90
demilitarized zone, 115
democracy, 13, 18, 32, 67, 71, 114
Democratic Republic of the Congo, 93
Deng Xiaoping, 108, 110
Denmark, 52
desalination, 74, 82

desert, 10, 18, 34, 44, 74, 77, 80, 85, 87–88, 90, 100, 106
desertification, 77, 90
developed countries, 16
developing countries, 16
dictatorship, 13, 71, 93, 114, 118
dike, 56
Djibouti, 96
Dominican Republic, 38
drought, 90, 96
drug trade, 43

E

earthquake, 6, 34, 113
East Asia, 59, 106, 113
East Germany, 55
economic systems, 13, 20, 32, 98
economy, mixed, 52, 66
ecosystems, 10, 18, 32, 47, 63, 70, 74, 85, 100, 106
Ecuador, 44
Egypt, 79, 85, 87–88
Elbe River, 55
embargo, 81
enclave, 98
England, 49–51. *See also* Britain, Great Britain.
entrepreneur, 67
Equator, 9–10, 85, 95, 106
Eritrea, 96
erosion, 7
escarpment, 40, 85
Estonia, 68
estuary, 45
Ethiopia, 96
ethnic groups, 29, 56, 63, 67, 72, 76–77, 79, 92, 96, 106, 110, 117–118
ethnocracy, 96
Eurasia, 63, 71
Europe, 21, 29, 47, 51, 54–55, 57, 59, 61, 63, 65–67, 70, 79–80, 85, 88, 91, 120
European Union, 47, 56, 60

F

farming, 16, 20, 23–25, 34–35, 38, 41, 43–44, 49, 55–57, 59–61, 66, 76–77, 81, 85, 88, 90, 95, 103–104, 106, 108–109, 111, 113, 117, 121
favelas, 40–41
federation, 13
Fertile Crescent, 74
Finland, 52
fishing, 26, 28, 43, 50, 61, 82, 121
fjords, 52
Flemings, 56
Florida, 24
forest, 10, 18, 20, 24, 26, 28, 32, 41, 44, 63, 70, 90, 93, 95, 106, 117

fossil fuels, 15, 18, 20
Four Modernizations, 108
France, 29, 51, 54, 71, 88, 118
free enterprise, 20
French Guiana, 43
French Revolution, 54
French Riviera, 54
Fulani, 92

G

Gandhi, Mohandas, 102
gauchos, 45
Gaza Strip, 80
Genghiz Khan, 111
Georgia, 76
geography, themes of, 5
geology, 6
geothermal energy, 15, 52
Germany, 49, 54–55, 114
geyser, 121
Ghana empire, 90
ghettoes, 65
glacier, 7, 52
glasnost, 71
Gobi Desert, 109, 111
government, 13, 29–30, 32, 35, 37, 41, 56, 63, 71, 77, 87, 91, 98, 103, 109, 111, 114, 118
grain exchange, 25
Gran Chaco, 45
grassland, 10, 18, 45, 63, 70, 77, 95, 106
Great Britain, 18, 49–50, 79, 122. *See also* Britain, England.
Great Dividing Range, 120
Great Lakes, 25, 28
Great Leap Forward, 108
Great Plains, 25
Great Rift Valley, 95
Greater Antilles, 38
Greece, 61, 83, 120
Gross Domestic Product (GDP), 16, 41
Gross National Product (GNP), 20
growing season, 25
Guadalquivir River, 59
guerrilla movement, 37
Guianas, 43
Gulf of Aden, 96
Guyana, 43

H

Haiti, 38
hajj, 82
Han ethnic group, 110
harambee, 95
Hausa, 92
Hawaii, 26
Hidalgo, Miguel, 35
hierarchy, 21
Himalayas, 100, 104
Hindu Kush, 104
Hinduism, 100, 117
Hindus, 102–103
Hispaniola, 38
Hitler, Adolf, 55
Ho Chi Minh, 118
Hokkaido, 113

Holocaust, 65
Hong Kong, 111
Honshu, 113
Horn of Africa, 96
Houston, Texas, 24
Huang He River, 109
Hudson Bay Lowland, 28
Hungary, 66
hurricane, 32, 113
Hussein (king of Jordan), 81
Hutu, 96
hydroelectric (power), 41, 45, 87, 104

I

Iberian Peninsula, 47, 59
Ibo, 92
Iceland, 52
ideogram, 110
Illinois, 25
immigration, 23, 29, 38, 51, 120
Inca, 32
India, 100, 102–104, 117
Indian Ocean, 100, 104, 106
Indiana, 25
Indians, 37, 40, 44, 102–103
Indonesia, 118
Indus River, 104
Industrial Revolution, 47, 49
industry, high-tech, 50, 56, 80, 103
industry, space, 24
industry, textile, 102
inflation, 55
infrastructure, 82
International Monetary Fund, 92
Inuit, 29
Iowa, 25
Iran, 82–83
Iraq, 81–82
Ireland, 51
Irkutsk, Russia, 63
iron ore, 49, 54–55, 57
irrigation, 34, 77, 80, 82, 103–104
Islam, 74, 76–77, 79, 82–83, 87, 100, 104, 117
Israel, 79–80, 87
isthmus, 37
Itaipu Dam, 45
Italy, 54, 60, 88, 120

J

Jamaica, 38
Japan, 106, 108, 113–115
Jerusalem, 74
Jews, 55, 65, 79, 80
Jordan, 79–81
Judaism, 74

K

Kansas, 25
Kara Kum, 77
Kazakhstan, 77
Kemal, Mustafa, 83
Kenya, 95
Kenyatta, Jomo, 95

Khan, Reza, 83
Kiev, Ukraine, 71
Kikuyu, 95
Kinshasa, Congo Republic, 93
Korea, 114
Kuwait, 81–82
Kyrgyzstan, 77
Kyzyl Kum, 77

L

land redistribution, 35
languages
    Afrikaans, 97
    Arabic, 79, 87–88
    Dutch, 56
    English, 29, 50
    Finnish, 52
    Flemish, 56
    French, 29, 54, 56–57
    Gaelic, 51
    German, 56–57
    Hindi, 100
    Italian, 57
    Luxembourgish, 56
    Mandarin, 110
    Romanian, 68
    Spanish, 44
    Welsh, 50
Latin America, 32, 59
Latvia, 68
League of Nations, 79
Lebanon, 81
Lena River, 70
Lesotho, 98
Lesser Antilles, 38
Liberia, 91
Libya, 88
literacy, 18
Lithuania, 68
llanos, 43
location
    absolute, 5
    relative, 5
London, England, 49
Long March, 108
Los Angeles, California, 26
Lutheran Church, 52
Luxembourg, 56

M

Macedonia, 67
Madrid, Spain, 59
Maghreb countries, 88
Magyars, 66
Malawi, 98
Mali, 90
malnutrition, 95, 98
mandate, 79
Mandela, Nelson, 97
mantle, earth's, 6
manufacturing, 23, 25, 41, 54–55, 57, 66, 76, 88
Mao Zedong, 108, 110
Maori, 121
market economy, 13, 32, 72
Marseille, France, 54
Masai, 95
Massif Central, 54
Mauritania, 90
Maya, 34
Mecca, Saudi Arabia, 82

Medina, Saudi Arabia, 82
Mediterranean Sea, 54, 61, 74, 76, 87–88
megalopolis, 23
Meiji government, 114
Melanesia, 121
mestizos, 32, 37, 44–45
Mexican Revolution, 35
Mexico, 5, 34–35
Mexico City, Mexico, 34, 35
Miami, Florida, 24
Micronesia, 121
Middle East, 79, 96
migrant workers, 35, 98
minerals, 15, 23, 26, 28, 43–44, 49, 57, 70, 80, 90, 93, 96, 120
Mobutu Sese Seko, 93
Moldova, 68
monarchy, 13, 54, 71
Mongol empire, 71, 111
Mongolia, 111
monotheism, 74
moors, 50
Morocco, 88
Moscow, Russia, 71
Mount Everest, 104
Mozambique, 98
mulattoes, 43
Muslims, 74, 79, 81–83, 96, 102, 117
Myanmar, 118

N

Namibia, 98
national identity, 54, 65, 118
nationalism, 76
Nationalists, Chinese, 108, 111
Native Americans, 18, 24, 29, 32, 44
natural gas, 15, 20, 26, 28, 34, 49, 74, 77
natural resources, 16, 20, 23–26, 28, 30, 41, 43, 47, 90, 114–115
Nazis, 55, 65, 114
Negev Desert, 80
Nepal, 104
Netherlands, 56
New Orleans, Louisiana, 24
New Spain, 35
New York City, New York, 21, 26
New Zealand, 106, 121
Niger, 90
Nigeria, 92
Nile River, 85, 87
Normans, 51
North Atlantic Drift, 47
North European Plain, 47
North Island, 121
North Korea, 115
North Sea, 49, 50
North Vietnam, 118
Northern Ireland, 49, 51
Northwest Territories, 28
Norway, 52
nuclear energy, 15
Nunavut, 28

O

Ob River, 70
oil, 15, 20, 24–26, 28, 34–35, 41, 43, 45, 49–50, 68, 70, 74, 76–77, 81–83, 85, 88, 92, 96
Oklahoma, 24
Oman, 82
Ontario, 28
Organization of Petroleum Exporting Countries (OPEC), 82
Ottoman Empire, 79, 83
Ottoman Turks, 79
outback, 120

P

Pacific Ocean, 26, 30, 34, 37, 44, 106, 121
Pahlavi, Mohammed Reza, 83
Pakistan, 102, 104
Palestine, 79–80
Palestinian Liberation Organization (PLO), 80
Palestinians, 79–81
pampas, 32, 45
Panama Canal, 37
Paraguay, 45
Paris, France, 54
partition, 102
Patagonia, 45
Pearl Harbor, Hawaii, 114
peat, 51
peninsula, 34, 47, 52, 59–60, 82, 106
Pennsylvania, 23
People's Republic of China, 108. *See also* China.
perestroika, 71
permafrost, 70
Persians, 83
Peru, 44
pharaoh, 87
Philippines, 118
piedmont, 45
plate tectonics, 6
Plateau of Mexico, 34
Plateau of Tibet, 109
Po River valley, 60
Poland, 55, 65
polder, 56
pollution, 15, 30, 63, 66, 72, 74, 113
Polynesia, 121
population, 12, 13, 16, 20, 23, 26, 28–30, 44, 47, 60, 68, 71–72, 74, 76, 83, 85, 87, 97, 100, 103, 106, 108–110, 113, 121
population density, 12, 26
Portugal, 32, 59, 98
poverty, 35, 40, 71
precipitation, 9, 24, 100
Presbyterian Church, 50
privatization, 66, 68
Protestants, 51
province, 28–29
Prussia, 55
Puerto Rico, 38

pyramids, 87
Pyrenees Mountains, 59

Q

Qatar, 82
Quebec, 28–29

R

recession, 54
Red Sea, 87, 96
refugees, 80–81, 90, 96
religion, 12, 51, 57, 63, 65, 71, 74, 87, 96, 100, 110, 117
Renaissance, 60
reparations, 55
Republic of Ireland, 51
Republic of South Africa, 97, 98
reservoir, 87
Rhine River, 54–55
Rhône River, 54
Ring of Fire, 113
Rio de Janeiro, 40
Río de la Plata, 45
Rocky Mountains, 18, 26
Roman Catholic Church, 51, 60, 65, 118
Roman Empire, 60–61
Romania, 67–68
Rome, Italy, 60
Rub' al-Khali, 82
Ruhr Valley, 55
Russia, 63, 68, 70–72, 111, 114, 122
Russian Revolution, 71
Rwanda, 96

S

Sahara, 85, 88, 90–91, 93
Sahel, 90–91
St. Lawrence Lowlands, 28
sanctions, 97
São Paulo, 40
São Tomé and Príncipe, 93
Sardinia, 60
Saudi Arabia, 82
Scandinavian Peninsula, 47, 52
Scotland, 49–50
Seljuk Turks, 79
Seoul, South Korea, 115
separatism, 29
sertão, 40–41
service industry, 16, 41, 49, 56, 68, 74, 80
shah, 83
Shanghai, China, 109
shifting agriculture, 90
Shinto, 113
Siberia, 70, 72
Sicily, 60
Sierra Leone, 91
Sierra Madre, 34
Sierra Madre Occidental, 34
Sierra Madre Oriental, 34
Sierra Nevada, 26
Silk Road, 109
Singapore, 118
slavery, 32, 38, 40, 85, 102
Slavs, 71–72

Slovakia, 66
Slovenia, 67
solar energy, 15
Solidarity, 65
Somalia, 96
Songhai empire, 90
South Africa. *See* Republic of South Africa.
South America, 32, 40, 43–45
South Asia, 100, 102–104, 117
South Island, 121
South Korea, 115
South Vietnam, 118
Southeast Asia, 106, 117–118, 120
Southwest Asia, 15, 74, 80–81, 83, 85
sovereignty, 13
Soviet Union, 65–66, 68, 71, 80, 104, 115
Spain, 32, 59
Special Economic Zones, 109, 111
spheres of influence, 108
Sri Lanka, 104
standard of living, 18, 30, 56–57, 111, 115
steel, 41, 49, 55
steppes, 63, 77, 111
subcontinent, 100, 102
subsistence farming, 16, 35, 44, 85
Sudan, 96
Suez Canal, 87
Sunbelt, 24
Suriname, 43
Swaziland, 98
Sweden, 52
Switzerland, 57
Syr Darya River, 77
Syria, 81

T

taiga, 63
Taiwan, 111
Tajikistan, 77
Tanzania, 96
technology, 5, 25, 80, 108–109
telecommunication, 20
Tenochtitlán, 35
terrace, 106, 113
terrorists, 80
Texas, 24
Thailand, 117–118
Thames River, 49
Thar Desert, 100, 104
Tiananmen Square, 108
Tibet, 109
tourism, 24, 34–35, 38, 50, 54, 61, 67, 76–77, 121
trade, 13, 16, 23, 30, 55–56, 59, 61, 68, 74, 81–82, 85, 88, 90–91, 106, 109, 111, 115, 117
traditional economy, 13, 32
transportation, 20–21, 25, 59, 72, 93, 109
trust territories, 121
tundra, 10, 18, 26, 63, 70

Tunisia, 88
Turkey, 61, 76, 83
Turkmenistan, 77
Tutsi, 96
typhoon, 113

U

Uganda, 96
Ukraine, 68, 71
underdeveloped countries, 16
Union of Soviet Socialist Republics. *See* Soviet Union.
United Arab Emirates, 82
United Kingdom, 49–51
United Nations, 79, 81, 92–93, 111, 115
United States, 18, 20–21, 23–26, 30, 35, 43, 49, 51, 67, 81, 97, 108, 114–115, 118, 122
Ural Mountains, 70
urbanization, 12, 30, 85
Uruguay, 45
Uzbekistan, 77

V

Vancouver, Canada, 28
Vatican City, 60
Venezuela, 43, 82
Vienna, Austria, 57
Vietnam, 117–118
Vikings, 52, 71
volcano, 6, 34, 38, 52, 113, 121
Volga River, 70

W

Wales, 49–50
Walloons, 56
Washington, D.C., 23–24
water, 10, 15, 25–26, 49, 72, 74, 77, 80, 85, 87, 104, 109
weather, 9, 67
weathering, 7
West Bank, 80–81
West Germany, 55
women, 91, 100
World Bank, 92
World War I, 55, 57, 66–67, 74, 76, 79
World War II, 55, 65–66, 79, 108, 114–115, 118, 120–121

Y

Yangzi River, 109
Yemen, 82
Yenisey River, 70
Yoruba, 92
Yucatán Peninsula, 34
Yugoslavia, 67
Yukon, 28

Z

Zambia, 98
Zimbabwe, 98
Zionists, 79–80